THE POSTMAN OF NAGASAKI

By the same author

EARTH MY FRIEND
DUEL OF EAGLES
THE LAST EMPEROR
TIME AND CHANCE: AN AUTOBIOGRAPHY
THE SMALLEST PAWNS IN THE GAME
THE GIRL IN THE WHITE SHIP

THE POSTMAN
OF NAGASAKI

Peter Townsend

COLLINS
8 Grafton St, London W1
1984

William Collins Sons & Co. Ltd
London · Glasgow · Sydney · Auckland
Toronto · Johannesburg

British Library Cataloguing in Publication Data

Townsend, Peter
The postman of Nagasaki.
1. Sumiteru   2. Atomic bomb victims – Japan –
Biography   3. Antinuclear movement – Japan
I. Title
327.1'74   JX1962.S7/

First published 1984
Reprinted 1984
© Peter Townsend 1984

ISBN 0 00 217067 1

Photoset in Linotron Sabon by
Rowland Phototypesetting Ltd
Bury St Edmunds, Suffolk
Made and printed in Great Britain by
William Collins Sons & Co. Ltd, Glasgow

AUTHOR'S
ACKNOWLEDGEMENTS

On my first visit to Nagasaki in 1978, to do some research for an earlier book, I questioned two survivors who were children at the time of the A-bomb. It was a painful and moving interview, most sensitively handled by the interpreter, Mrs Rumiko Shimozuma, of the Nagasaki Prefecture Foreign Affairs Department. From her, I understood for the first time something of the agony of Nagasaki.

The idea of a story about Nagasaki came to me that day. On subsequent visits to the city and during the intervals between, the project, thanks to Rumiko's interest, slowly became reality. I am deeply indebted to her for her invaluable help and the warm hospitality of her home and family.

My researches in Nagasaki began early in 1982. The two big problems were, of course, language – which means interpreters – and witnesses – finding the ones who could tell me about all aspects of the A-bomb. In both these areas, the response of the people mentioned below was unreserved. I am particularly grateful to those who invited me to their homes or, in other ways, showed me such warm hospitality. During several weeks spent in Nagasaki, I walked for scores of kilometres, trammed, bussed and boated for hundreds more, in order to find these kind people and to follow up the information I had collected from them. At the end of it, I can say, with the millions of visitors who come yearly to the city: 'I love Nagasaki.'

I wish especially to thank the following:

In Tokyo (where the trail began):
  Mr Yukio Shimohira, Ministry of Health and Welfare.

Mr Nobuaki Oda, Information Officer, United Nations.
Mr Osamu Shiraishi, Programme Officer, United Nations High Commissioner for Refugees.
Miss Michiko Inukai, United Nations High Commissioner for Refugees.

In Nagasaki:

The Mayor, Mr Hitoshi Motoshima.
Mr Noboru Tasaki of the Mayor's Office, who arranged meetings with a wide variety of witnesses, and often accompanied me, as interpreter, on his days off.
Mr Miyaki Kagimoto, Director, Nagasaki International Cultural Hall, and his staff.
Doctor Tatsuichiro Akizuki, MD, Chief Medical Officer, St Francis Hospital.
Mrs Sugako Akizuki, his charming and talented wife, who as a nurse, was on the doctor's staff on A-bomb day. They married later.
Doctor Sadahisa Kawamoto, MD, Chief, Radiation Effects and Research Foundation, Nagasaki.
Professor S. Okajima, Nagasaki Medical School.
Doctor Nagatoshi Fujida, MD, Director, A-bomb Hospital (Genbaku Boyin), Nagasaki.
Mother Sachie Kawaguchi, Director, Junshin A-bomb Home of the Hill of Blessing.
Mr Takashi Ogawa, Director, Nagasaki Prefecture United Nations and Friendship Association.
Mr Terumasa Matsunaga, Deputy Chief for Peace Education, Municipal Board of Education, Nagasaki Prefecture.
Mr Hirosi, Nagasaki High Schools' Peace Seminar.
Mr Shinji Takahashi, PhD, Nagasaki College of Applied Science for his views on the psychological and material effects on A-bomb survivors.
Mr H. Hirose, lately of Mitsubishi Heavy Industries.

Father Joseph Aguilla, SJ, Director, Nagai Centre.

Father Diego Yuuki (Paceco), SJ, Director, 26 Martyrs Museum.

Father McAtie, Director, Augustinian Brothers' School.

The Reverend Yoshitada (John) Miyahara, Church of England.

The Most Reverend Yashiaki Kizu, Curate of the Goshin-Ji (Buddhist) temple, for their welcome and for their erudite views on the religious and moral issues concerning the atom bomb.

Mr Tokai, interpreter, Radiation Effects Research Foundation.

Mr Katsunobu Shiina, Kasei High School.

Mr Tetsuo Kiyomura.

Miss Kumiko Hashida.

Miss Miyuki Yamashita.

Miss Kuni Murakawa, who, responding to an appeal for interpreters, volunteered, giving up much of their spare time. I feel particularly touched by their generosity.

Mr Masato Araki, vice-director, International Cultural Hall.

Mr Senzi Yamaguti, president Nagasaki *Hibakusha* Association.

Miss Yukie Tsuji, founder member of the above association.

Mr Tadashi Kokurawa.

Yasuko, his daughter (second generation A-bombed).

Miss Mayumi Okabu, her friend (second generation A-bombed).

Mr Taisuki Hashiguchi (second generation, A-bombed), KTN TV, and many others whose testimonies were essential to the story.

And of course, Sumiteru Taniguchi and his wife Eiko, for their warm hospitality and the many hours they spent, during those hot, busy days and nights of August 1982, telling me the smallest details of their story.

Group Captain Leonard Cheshire, VC, who was good enough

to talk with me at length about 'The Nuclear Dilemma' and to give me a copy of his paper on the subject, in which he pleads the cause of the nuclear 'deterrent'. One of my objects in this book is to suggest that, if the deterrent is ever used, it will be the end of us and our planet, Earth.

Philip Ziegler, my editor at Collins, London, for his most helpful suggestions.

Dana Noyé, my daughter, Marie-Françoise, and my son, Pierre, all had a hand in typing the manuscript, filled as it is, with unfamiliar Japanese names and English technical terms. I thank them warmly for their painstaking work.

A final and heartfelt acknowledgement. It so happened that, hardly had I begun my researches in Nagasaki in April 1982, than I received news that one of my family was seriously ill. I am profoundly grateful to my friend Monsieur Henri Pigeat, director of Agence France Presse, Paris, and to Monsieur Bolo, the agency's correspondent in Tokyo, for their successful efforts in locating me.

I left Nagasaki next day, 6 April. Air France Flight 273 brought me home over the pole to Paris. I shall never forget the sympathy and the practical help shown to me by the staff of Air France on the ground at Osaka, Tokyo and Anchorage (Alaska), and by the flying and cabin crew, during the anxious hours of the long journey home. In August, I returned to Nagasaki.

I

Sumiteru Taniguchi was only one year old when his mother Kiku died. Though her disappearance had no meaning for him at the time it would later be heavy with consequence – not so much because it deprived him of her maternal care, as because his father, Sadamachi, took him and his brother and sister from their home at Fukuoka, on Kyushu, the most westerly of Japan's four main islands, to live with their grandmother in Nagasaki, sixty kilometres away. Sadamachi then got a job on the railways in Manchuria, the furthest-flung province of the Japanese empire, and he too disappeared out of the life of his young family. It was left to their grandmother to rear the three children: Keiko, then a girl of seven, Teiji, a three-year-old boy and the infant Sumiteru.

Nagasaki was unlike any other town in Japan. It was a port; in 1570, three and a half centuries before Sumiteru arrived, Portuguese ships had put in there. From Holland, China, England and Spain came more ships and in the wake of the seamen and traders there followed Franciscan and Jesuit missionaries; among them one of the greatest in all Christendom, Francis Xavier. Though Buddism had reached Japan from China centuries earlier that did not deter the Christian missionaries from preaching salvation through Jesus Christ to the Japanese.

They had gathered many sheep into the fold when, in 1579, the Japanese government reacted. Twenty-six Christians, missionaries and Japanese converts were condemned to death. On Nishizaka, a hill in Nagasaki facing the harbour, each martyr was hoisted on a cross, then run through by the spears of the soldiery. The massacre only brought more converts to Christianity.

Infuriated by their zeal, the Shoguns, Japan's feudal rulers, ordered further killings. The soil of Nishizaka ran with the blood of hundreds more Christians until, banned altogether in the mid-seventeenth century, the church went underground. During the next two hundred years, the Christian message was passed on by word of mouth, from generation to generation.

Meanwhile, by command of the shogunate, Japan was cut off from the outside world. Foreigners living there were expelled and all others forbidden, on pain of death, to enter. Only one port in the whole country was exempted from the order: Nagasaki. A few Dutch and Chinese traders were allowed to stay on and for the next two centuries, while the rest of Japan remained rooted in feudal law and customs, Nagasaki flourished. Thanks to its continuing contact with Asia and the West, foreign culture and science, technology and consumer goods had access to the port.

It was not until the mid-nineteenth century, with the accession of the emperor Meiji – 'enlightened Rule' – that Japan began to emerge from isolation and feel the impact of the West. In Nagasaki, Christianity came out from the shades and re-established itself in the form of the beautiful wooden gothic Church of the Twenty-six Martyrs, on the hillside at Oura, overlooking the harbour. Now that other ports became accessible Nagasaki had to surrender its exclusive relationship with the West. The Dutch and Chinese lost their special privileges as traders from other nations installed themselves in the city. However, business flourished; in 1859 a British consulate was established – in a temple, for want of other accommodation.

In Nagasaki, that year will be more remembered for the arrival of a twenty-one-year-old Scot, Thomas Blake Glover. Some say that no man contributed more to the modernization of Japan. Through his initiative young Japanese were sent to Britain, where they studied everything from the constitution to the building of ships. If Glover's ties were closest with Mitsubishi, industries as varied as coal-mining, coin-minting and the railways all profited from his enterprise. Thanks to him, too, the English rose made its début in Japan and his Japanese wife, a talented artist, familiarized the West with her paintings of that exquisite species of flora surnamed 'Japonica'.

Close to the Church of the Twenty-six Martyrs, Glover built a mansion, surrounding it with a spacious garden. From there, on the hillside at Oura, he could survey the comings and goings of the ships and merchandise which were the source of his fortune. When he moved to Tokyo, it was as adviser to Mitsubishi, the driving force of Nagasaki's industry.

Considering all that Glover had done for Japan – or more exactly because of it – the fate of his son, when war came, was to be a cruel one. Oddly enough, it was in some way bound up with the fate of Sumiteru.

2

Half way down the steep slope of Mount Inasa, the highest of all the green hills which descend upon Nagasaki and its harbour, there stood, in the early thirties, a small wooden house. It was the home of Sumiteru's grandmother, Taga, whom the children called Oba-chan. In future it was to be their home as well and Inasa, with its varying moods, a presence and an influence in their lives.

Mount Inasa, considering its altitude of only 330 metres, hardly deserves to be called a mountain, but it is the only prominent summit jutting up from the line of hills on the western side of the long valley in which Nagasaki lies. Towards the east, the hills climb to other summits, the most graceful being Konpira, but Inasa has no rival, least of all when the rays of the setting sun are diffused behind its darkening silhouette. There are few places in that elongated city from which Inasa is not visible; it is the hill most familiar to the citizens of Nagasaki and the most loved. From the top of Inasa, the view takes in the whole of Nagasaki, from the harbour entrance northwards to the head of the valley where the town dwindles away. To the east, beyond Mount Konpira, the skyline is punctuated by other heights: Tenjiku, and Hoba, Hoka, Atago and Hoshitoriyama, the 'star-gatherer' – a spectacular panorama of tree-clad hills with the city and its long, narrow harbour enclosed among them.

Nagasaki lay exactly north-south along two main axes: the Urakami river and a long, straight road which was nameless, like all other roads and streets in Nagasaki, but identified as 'Route 206'. Down from the hills in the north the Urakami flowed into the city through a pleasant valley where Christians congregated and built, with their own hands, an imposing cathedral; it took them thirteen years. The Urakami river then changed into a nondescript water course, its banks reinforced with stone, for when swollen with heavy rain, it would come hurtling down, bringing with it débris, which might include carts and motor-cars from flooded homes upstream.

In Nagasaki city, the residential areas, with their establishment of hospitals and schools, stood back from the river, reaching up into narrow valleys towards the higher ground; peaceful and pleasant enclaves whose streets in April were adorned with the frail pink of cherry blossom and where, during the hot, humid summer days, the air vibrated with the ceaseless pulsating of a million cicadas. Strung out along the floor of the valley were factories working day and night, turning out weapons and merchandise for Japan and its empire; the biggest of them displayed the red triple-diamond symbol of Mitsubishi Heavy Industries. On the northern outskirts of the town, tucked away into tunnels bored into the chalky hillside, was the Mitsubishi torpedo factory, concealed from the air. A little further down the valley where the river, flanked by rice fields, swung south to begin its run through the town, the vast hangars of the company's ordnance factory and the ship-testing tank were ranged methodically on the right bank. Through mid-town the Urakami ran on past the Mitsubishi shipyard factory, the electrical plant, and the steel works with their rows of tall chimneys. A couple of hundred metres away, Urakami station was the last stop on the main line before the terminus at Nagasaki; there, where the train finally stopped, the Urakami river ended too, emptying itself into the harbour. More rail tracks led on from the terminus down to Ohato pier and the docks on the harbour's eastern seaboard, where the ground rose gently out of the Urakami basin to slope down again towards a smaller river, the Niyashima.

This was down-town Nagasaki: quays and warehouses cluttered with merchandise, streets crowded with shops and shoppers, strongholds of local government, like the prefecture

15

and the city hall and, within a stone's throw, the main post office with postmen on red bicycles coming and going, and the fire station, its red engines and shiny-helmeted crews loitering beside them, waiting for action.

Opposite the down-town area, a kilometre away across the harbour, an array of cranes and gantries advertised the presence of the greatest of Mitsubishi's enterprises – its shipyard. Long hulls, still building, were shored up in dock and others anchored off-shore, elegant monsters beside the stumpy trawlers of the fishing fleet moored at an adjacent quay. Downtown Nagasaki rambled on beyond the docks and along the shore until, abruptly, the scene changed on the rising ground at Oura, upon which stood the Church of the Twenty-six Martyrs and, adjoining it, the splendid mansions built decades ago by Glover and his foreign friends. Against the Japanese landscape they looked as outlandish as did the charming gothic church next door and the Urakami cathedral at the other end of the town. But they left on Nagasaki a certain exotic imprint which distinguished it from other Japanese towns. It was natural that Nagasaki, so beautiful and with its centuries-old associations with Western civilization, should be considered as a town apart; unthinkable that it would one day, in a fraction of a second, be reduced to ashes by a Western power.

3

This was the city where Sumiteru had come to live and the time would come when he would get to know it street by street. Until then he was raised on a hill, close to the earth and the sky, an environment which would create in him, as it did in every other creature living on the hill, a strong instinct for survival. But in his grandmother Oba-chan's house he could never feel far from the city below. On clear days it was easy to pick out the main landmarks in down-town Nagasaki and on the hill at Oura. Immediately below, a few cranes poked out from behind the hill which hid the rest of the Mitsubishi dockyard.

It was easy to distinguish the ferry-boats plying the harbour, the big steamers berthed at the docks, and even the black and yellow colour of the fishing boats. Occasionally, the moaning of a ship's siren resounded up on the hill at Oba-chan's home.

A narrow path led down from the house into Nagasaki; somehow avoiding the steepest declivities, it would here and there break into a flight of steps where the slope became too forbidding. There were 150 steps on the way down and of course, on the way up, which was a more serious matter.

Above the house the sheerness of the high ground was to some extent camouflaged by a jungle of unkempt trees and creeper, from which emerged every now and then a clump of tall bamboos looking like ostrich feathers when ruffled by the wind. As the down-gradient eased and the slopes began to lengthen there arose a forest of dark-green pine growing wild except where men, bettering nature, had planted trees, taller and straighter, in long conventional rows. In spring, wild azalea spurted like flame on the hill and rock – orchids and camellia blossomed in the valleys. On the lower fringe of the forest some of the ground had been cleared and a few isolated holdings, like Oba-chan's, clung to the slope. Then the hills rolled on, some down to the shoreline, others into the distance where they merged with the sky. There were no confines either to the space or the beauty of Sumiteru's new habitat.

Sumiteru's grandmother Oba-chan and her late husband had raised their own family up there on the hill. Their small plot of land, their chickens, rabbits and silkworms, provided the basic means of survival and the occasional sale of surplus products brought in a few much-needed *yen*. It had been a hard struggle and now that her husband and her daughter, Sumiteru's mother, were dead and the other children dispersed, there could still be no let-up for Oba-chan. The arrival of her daughter's children meant further ceaseless toil and responsibility. But the children brought her welcome company and the promise of help in extracting from the grudging soil the food which formed the greater part of their diet: soya beans, maize and potatoes, tomatoes, cucumbers and water melons; rice was bought at a local shop. A corner was kept for chrysanthemums too; they were for fêtes and funerals. The added numbers in Oba-chan's household furnished another essential element: manure. Nothing was more effective than human excreta.

Keiko, though only seven, was put to work out of school hours; she now wore the blue uniform dress of the Asahi *shoga-ko*, the elementary school, some minutes' walk down the hill. Her lessons finished, she would return to help with the chores of the house and the land. Oba-chan taught her to cook on the *kudo*, a brick stove fired with wood which the little girl herself had to gather on the hillside. It was hard for her at first, for her grandmother was a severe taskmistress, but Oba-chan was not unkind and Keiko gradually fell in with her rigorous ways. 'Sumi-chan', as they affectionately called Sumiteru, would never forget how strict she was with him and his brother Teiji, '*Oni-chan*'. But the brothers would never forget either how fondly their sister mothered them; they called her 'Onéchan' and could always rely on her when Oba-chan was in a bad temper.

Teiji was five when he, too, was enlisted in the family work-force; Oba-chan gave him the job of feeding the chickens and rabbits; the silkworms fed themselves on the leaves of the mulberry trees growing round the house. Back-breaking jobs like hoeing, weeding and wood-gathering began to come his way. Never far from his brother's side, Sumi-chan in time took naturally to the same work. The boys' area was strictly out of doors; Oba-chan would not have them meddling inside the house – cooking, laundering and spinning silk were skilled tasks reserved for herself and Keiko.

One day – Sumi-chan must have been about five – Teiji took him by the hand and, leading him beyond the fields, made for the forest. There lived the *mejiro*, the most beautiful bird on the hill, green all over with a white circle round each eye and the prize of bird-fanciers, including Teiji and Sumiteru, who kept five of them in bamboo cages made by themselves. During their expeditions on the hillside, they gathered food for their pets: yellow-petalled *kuchinashi*, and the fluffy heads of *tampopo*, dandelions gone to seed. Above them *karusu*, buzzards, soared gracefully, safely beyond their reach, though they could hear their cry, a high-pitched *kawayi, kawayi*. The word in Japanese means 'lovely' and the boys would remember the old song:

> *Karusu, karusu*, why do you cry
> since you have so many lovely children
> in the mountain.

For the pot, the boys were always after the *hyo*, a grey-brown bird, fleshy and good to eat, and the sparrows which flitted round the house. All means to ensure their death or capture were fair, if not always legal: bird-lime, decoys, catapult or a well-aimed stone. Sumiteru became the best marksman; young as he was he had the instincts of a hunter, combining a lively sense of adventure and of self-preservation; the latter was to save him from many a violent brush with his grandmother when those expeditions on the hillside with his brother became longer and more frequent. Not that Oba-chan worried about them, but she was angry when they did not turn up in time to feed the animals or eat their meal. She would wait for them, ready to mete out punishment, but Sumiteru was nearly always too quick for her; taking to his heels he would shin up the tall persimmon tree just down the slope or, failing that, scramble down the cliffside beyond. It was poor Teiji, less fleet of foot, who was often caught and spanked.

But Oba-chan, for all her wrathful outbursts, was fond of the boys and not displeased when they brought back a bird or two for the pot. It all helped, and she would allow them, with Keiko helping, to grill them outside on the *shochirin*, a cylindrical charcoal stove; the smell of burning charcoal would for ever remind Sumiteru of those good days on the hill alone with Teiji, or playing hide and seek with his classmates from the Asahi *shoga-ko* and vying with them in races and tests of endurance. Sumiteru had few equals, which was all the more astonishing because of his size. He was shorter than any of the sixty pupils in his class, yet more verve and energy seemed to be condensed in his small person than in all the others. They adopted him as their mascot.

If Sumiteru revelled in the discipline of the hill, he took less easily to that of the classroom. He teased the girls and shut them out, and the tricks he played on his teachers earned him many a long wait in the corner or up on the roof. Once, when sent up to stand on the roof, his teacher forgot him and went home; it was not until evening that he was discovered still up there by the caretaker. Sumiteru refused to come down without the personal permission of his teacher who, called to the spot, had to concede that his obstinate little pupil had won the day.

Sumiteru was certainly no bookworm, but he somehow managed to cope with his lessons. Among them, history had a vital place. In recent years, Japanese history had been eventful, to say the least. Not that the class were taught any more than the rudiments; the chief lesson to be drawn was, as the old

Meiji slogan went, 'Rich country, strong army'. Japan never lost any battles.

Certainly, Japan had come a long way since the time when Glover had arrived in Nagasaki. Her industry had copied and often improved on the techniques imported from the West. She possessed a powerful army and navy which between them, at the turn of the century, had beaten both the Chinese and Russians in war. Japan was master of Formosa and Korea, and in the southern part of the rich Chinese province of Manchuria her industry was beginning to flourish and her Kwantung Army kept order.

If Japan had the makings of an empire, things were far from well at home. Business and politics were riddled with corruption; the politicians were distrusted by the military who, with their access to the Emperor, could topple the government when they pleased; their power was great and they intended to increase it.

Abroad meanwhile, the Western powers were discriminating against oriental countries. Japanese exports did not sell, and food imports, sorely needed to feed an exploding population, could not be paid for. When economic depression hit the world in 1929, the year that Sumiteru was born, Japan was facing starvation. Emigration seemed to be the solution; Manchuria the promised land, the land of plenty.

But Manchuria had to be won – by force – from the Chinese. The process had already begun with the murder of the Chinese governor in 1928, by Japanese troops. The Japanese Prime Minister Hamaguchi, who had tried to curb the militarists, was assassinated two years later; then, in 1931, the Kwantung Army picked a quarrel with the Chinese and occupied the key city of Mukden. Within a few months the whole of Manchuria was in Japanese hands, and Japanese money and immigrants began pouring in. Sumiteru's father, Sadamachi, was one of the pioneers.

The 'Manchurian incident' was followed a year later, by the 'Shanghai incident' in which Japanese naval officers tried to lift a boycott in the port against their country's goods. Ignored by the government, the more frustrated of them returned to Tokyo and murdered the Prime Minister, Inukai. Biding their time, the military waited until February 1936; then, while Tokyo lay beneath the snow, an army unit revolted and killed a number of leading politicians. At the end of that year, Japan sided with the two European aggressor nations, Germany and Italy, in the anti-Comintern pact against Russia. On the strength of that, less than a year later, she provoked yet another 'incident', the 'China incident' which started an atrocious and exhausting eight-year war with China.

These details never reached the innocent ears of young Sumiteru. All he ever heard was that in China, Japan was always winning, and that in Europe her allies Germany and Italy, were winning, too. By mid-1940, he heard they had won completely – except against Britain, the ally of America. Both these countries, explained Sumiteru's teacher, were enemies of Japan, because they were trying to dominate the world and Japan in particular, preventing her from becoming a rich and powerful nation. But Japan and her two great allies would surely win in time, against them too. Meanwhile she wasted no time in cashing in on Germany's defeat of France; the French colony of Indo-China, with all its riches, was there for the taking. For a start, Japan built air bases in the north of Indo-China, for stepping up her attacks on China; a year later, in July 1941, without a murmur of dissent from the French government, her troops occupied the entire country. It was a deft thrust at her enemies, the white colonial powers – America in the Philippines, Britain in Hong Kong, Burma, Malaya and Singapore, and the Dutch, who still ruled in the East Indies. As far as Sumiteru could tell, this proved that Japan was, as always, winning.

What Sumiteru's teacher did not mention was that Japan's aggression against China, stained as it was by the hideous atrocities committed by her army, had been condemned universally, even by Germany, but particularly by America, Japan's chief source of oil. Now that she had seized Indo-China, the American President Franklin Roosevelt (whom the

Japanese, unable to pronounce the consonants 'R' and 'V', called Loosebelt) shut off the oil and froze Japanese assets; Britain and Holland did likewise. This, in the mind of the Japanese Government, was almost an act of war – and there was no lack of military extremists in Japan who relished the prospect, even if there was a possibility that it might end in national *hara-kiri*, suicide.

Now that Japan was so well poised to reap the riches of the 'white' colonies, including unlimited supplies of oil, there seemed no reason why she should not keep on winning – so long as she started the war without delay, for oil reserves were running low. She accelerated her preparations for war, her spies reconnoitred the enemy terrain in the minutest detail and contacted subversive elements which, among the Asians at that time, were not hard to find. All this, while her envoys in Washington, Nomura and Kisuru, friends of America and men of good will, continued to search for a diplomatic settlement with America's high-minded, stiff-necked Secretary of State, Cordell Hull. Throughout the talks, which lasted for months, every message between the Japanese in Tokyo and in Washington was intercepted by American intelligence. Unfortunately most were mistranslated, giving Hull the impression that the Japanese envoys were basely lulling him with talk of peace while Japan was intent on war. This was not essentially true – there were men in the Japanese Government who genuinely sought peace. But there were others, military fanatics, who were convinced that the destiny of Japan, land of the gods, lay in war. The talks in Washington were futile and sometimes bitter, but nothing like as bitter as the heated shouting matches between the militarists and the moderates of the Cabinet in Tokyo.

Only when the Emperor presided at cabinet meetings did his august presence ensure calm. A studious, frugal man, entirely free of ambition, he was revered as a deity and the father of the nation, to which he was selflessly devoted. He remained above politics, but by warning or approving nevertheless exercised great influence. He distrusted the military who had become a law to themselves; the Emperor called them 'stupid'. His own feelings on the present crisis were expressed in a poem, written by his grandfather, the Emperor Meiji, which he read out during an imperial conference:

> All the seas everywhere
> Are brothers to one another.
> Why then do the winds and waves of strife
> Rage so violently through the world?

The Prime Minister, Prince Konoye, cultured and intelligent but, in his own words, a 'lazy-bones', was against the use of force. 'It's obvious that you'll have to give up the idea of starting war,' he coolly told the military Chiefs of Staff. Finance Minister Kaya was also ardently in favour of peaceful negotiations, and when he heard that the military advised these should be kept going while they made ready for war, objected angrily that, after 2600 years of history when the fate of Japan hung in the balance, it was outrageous to resort to diplomatic trickery. Kido, keeper of the Privy Seal, and the Emperor's trusted personal adviser, was a wise and moderate man. Rather than go to war, he told the Cabinet the people should be warned that they now faced ten to fifteen years of *gashin-shotan*, meaning literally 'sleeping on kindling and licking gall' – in other words, hard times. Foreign Minister Toyoda hoped that problems would be settled in a calm and friendly atmosphere; his successor, Togo, begged for time to negotiate, to which the army men replied in so many words, 'If the Foreign Minister opposes war, all we have to do is to replace him.'

All these peace-seeking ministers were civilians, but it was another civilian, Matsuoka, one-time Foreign Minister, who had said at the outset of the discussions, 'We must either shed blood or embark on diplomacy. It's better to shed blood.' This was the kind of talk that pleased the military extremists, steeped as they still were in the *samurai* warrior tradition and obedient to its code, *bushido*, with its ultimate act of honour, *hara-kiri*, suicide by disembowelment – the traditional way of 'apologizing' to the Emperor.

Yet not all the military were whole-heartedly for war – at least to begin with. Army Chief of Staff Sugiyama wavered – no doubt in deference to the emperor, to whom he said, 'We'd rather not fight at all.' As the debate warmed up, however, he was insisting that war was the only answer. His Vice-Chief Tsukuda was never in two minds. 'We must go to war,' he cried. 'We will build an iron wall and inside it will crush our Asiatic enemies. We will also crush America and Britain.' War Minister General Tojo agreed: 'We must crush Britain.' The Navy, though traditionally more reasonable and cautious, were ready to fight – they were running short of oil. Chief of Staff Admiral Nagano's view was that Japan had better take the initiative. 'We will win,' he added confidently. Asked when Japan should go to war, he snapped, 'At once.' The Admiral added: 'If we don't fight, wouldn't that be the same as losing the war?'

Weeks of fruitless argument led Prince Konoye, in desperation, to resign the premiership in mid-October 1941. General Tojo took over; he enjoyed great prestige with the Army and was known to be war-minded. But he now resolved to think as a civilian, not as a soldier; 'I have no desire for war,' he announced, and complained that the military were meddling too much. Tojo was torn between the Emperor's desire for peace and his own instinct as a soldier to fight: 'I am praying to the gods,' he said, 'that in some way we'll come to an agreement with the Americans.' Yet simultaneously he wondered how long the people could endure *gashin-shotan*. 'We shall become a third-class nation if we just sit tight,' was his conclusion.

In Washington, the talks were getting nowhere. Cordell Hull thought Tojo was just a 'typical Japanese officer with a small-bore, straight-laced, one track mind'. He called him stupid, but Hull, judging by his high-handed dealings with the two Japanese envoys, may well have been just as stupid himself. A last plea for peace came from President Roosevelt. In a long cable to the Japanese Emperor he concluded '... both of us have a sacred duty to restore traditional amity and prevent further death and destruction in the world'.

Such were the men who debated the vital issue, war or peace – the elect and the all-powerful in whose hands lay the fate of the ordinary people, young Sumiteru among them, boys and girls and all the rest as innocent as he. The trouble with the top men was that they saw the people whose destiny they sought to shape as an anonymous mass or a bunch of statistics, not as private persons with private lives and feelings which could be pleased or hurt and who were practically defenceless against the engines of war loosed against them by the men at the top. It was they, the little folk, and not the armed forces, who ultimately were the pawns in the game being played out in Tokyo and Washington.

To Sumiteru, up on the hill, those great men were just names, most of them hardly heard of – except for the Emperor, godhead of the divine state-family, for whom Sumiteru, like every Japanese alive, was pledged to die if need be. But godhead? Sumiteru was not quite sure; a Buddhist by faith, he frankly felt closer to God on the hill. Nor did the rumours of war and of the expansion of the empire, which reached him through the bellicose dissertations of his history teacher, do anything to excite his enthusiasm for war. Life as it was gave him all he could wish for.

Down below in Nagasaki city, however, the exhortations of ministers and government officials were stirring up fervour for the divine person of the Emperor. The clamour for war was mounting; Japan, people were urged, now faced the greatest crisis in her long history. Her cause was righteous: to defend her empire, won at such great cost in blood and money, and to free herself and a thousand million other Asiatics from the yoke of white domination. A new patriotic song, broadcast by Tokyo radio, made an immediate hit. It began:

Siren, siren, air raid, air raid
What is that to us?
Enemy planes are only mosquitoes or dragonflies.

Amidst all this bravado, the public, including school-children, were being conscripted to build air-raid shelters; at Nagasaki, many were tunnelled into the hillside, and air-raid drills were teaching people the tactics of fighting fire, the dread of every Japanese city, with its wooden houses.

It was the prevailing mood, no doubt, which gave more atmosphere than usual to that year's Obon, the Buddhist festival of the dead, who are believed to return home and visit the living. During the three days that the feast lasts, from the 12th to the 15th August, the whole family is involved. They erect a frail wooden trellis above the tomb, adorned with chrysanthemums and messages. There they kneel in prayer, parents and children, and lay their offerings of flowers and food; that done, they sit around reminiscing happily about their departed loved ones. Back at home, everyone helps in building the boat, mounted on a light, wheeled chassis in which, on the last night of Obon, the spirits of the dead will be launched out to sea to make their journey back to their eternal abode.

Sumiteru's ancestors were buried at Nagayo, some kilometres away beyond the Nagasaki valley, but he had a friend whose family tomb was in the Buddhist cemetery on the hillside below Oba-chan's home. It is the custom in Japan to help bereaved neighbours; Sumiteru brought chrysanthemums from his grandmother's garden and wild flowers he had gathered on the hillside; he helped the family to build their boat and deck it out with photos and flowers and sprigs of fir. Every night he would sit on the hillside listening to the crackle of fireworks in the valley below and watching the rockets which came darting up to explode in a shower of coloured stars. When the great day, the fifteenth, came, Sumiteru was one of the band of youngsters, all clad in white, who helped trundle the boat bearing the spirits of the dead down the hill towards the harbour side. They made their way slowly through the thronged streets of Nagasaki, throwing fire-crackers which burst in their path, half deafening the on-lookers and choking them with smoke.

Hundreds of boats converging down-town on Route 206, formed into a cortège which forged on through the din and smoke of fire-crackers and the jubilant crowds, to the quayside next to the Ohato pier. There, instead of being launched directly upon the waters, each boat, flowers, photos and all, was seized by a mechanical grab and deposited in the hold of a ship moored alongside. Those beautiful boats, their lamented cargo notwithstanding, could not be allowed to clutter up Nagasaki's busy harbour; transported beyond it, they were dumped on the high seas. It came to the same thing in the end.

Obon was over; the din ceased, the smoke died away. Municipal work-gangs were already clearing the streets of débris and the happy crowds were making their way home. Sumiteru and his friends climbed the path and the 150 steps and each one returned to his home on the hill.

That day, in Urakami cathedral, in the Church of the Twenty-six Martyrs and other churches too, Christians had also been celebrating. It was the Feast of the Assumption.

A hundred or so kilometres up the coast from Nagasaki, navy torpedo-bombers were daily scaring the life out of the inhabitants of the coastal town of Kagoshima. After scraping over the peak of a 5000-foot mountain, they would throttle back and dive down, dodging chimneys and telegraph poles, to flatten out a few feet above the harbour. Steadying their aircraft, they would go through the motions of launching a torpedo on an imaginary target; then, 'wave-chopping', they would beat a hurried retreat from the vicinity. It was fun for the navy aircrews, but they knew no better than the infuriated inhabitants of Kagoshima what the object of this noisy, hair-raising exercise might be. The eventual target was known only to the planners at supreme headquarters.

The Emperor was aroused from his sleep to be presented with Roosevelt's message. It had arrived too late, not that it would have changed anything. At 7.30 a.m. on 8 December (it was still the 7th in the United States) loudspeakers blared in every town in Japan announcing that the nation was at war with

America and Britain. Some hours earlier Japanese Navy planes from the carrier striking force *Kido Butai* had attacked the US Pacific Fleet anchored in 'Battleship Row', Pearl Harbor. Those dare-devil 'dummy' attacks at Kagoshima had paid off handsomely; the navy pilots had sunk or damaged more than half of the Pacific Fleet.

Simultaneously with the attack on Pearl Harbor, powerful Japanese forces landed on the northeast coast of the British colony, Malaya, to begin a relentless drive south on Singapore, the 'impregnable' island fortress, six hundred kilometres south. Singapore was bombed early that morning; a few hours later a mass raid by Japanese bombers and fighters crippled the US Far East Air Force at Clark Field, north of Manila in the Philippines.

That morning, at school, Sumiteru joined in the general rejoicing; what else could he do? On his history teacher's portable radio, he heard Prime Minister Tojo say that the West was trying to dominate the world and that the enemy must be annihilated. Then came the strains of the well-known song,

> Across the sea, corpses in the water
> Across the mountain, corpses in the field
> I shall die for the Emperor
> I shall never look back.

Sumiteru shuddered. The class was dismissed and straight-away he walked out, alone, on the hill, wondering why on earth he should ever have to fight anyone. The words of the song come back to him. 'Across the mountain' had never meant corpses and death to him; it had always meant life and fun.

By noon that day, the Emperor had put his seal on the document declaring war. It concluded with an allusion to 'the glory of our empire'.

In forty years, Japan had won for itself a sizeable empire; it extended from Manchuria in the north, included large parts of China and reached to Indo-China in the south. Formosa and Korea were its two most ancient possessions; the former an island outpost close to the whites' colonial territories in the south. Korea, ruthlessly subjugated and plundered, was a source of manpower. Countless lusty young Koreans were shipped across the 150 kilometres of the Tsujima strait to Japan, there to be used as cannon-fodder for the Army or to do the donkey-work in Japanese industry. Thousands of them worked in Nagasaki.

Among the Japanese colonists living in Korea was a builder, Saichi, and his family from Noda, a pretty hamlet of Togitsu, a fishing village not far north of Nagasaki. He rented a small house in the suburbs of Seoul, the Korean capital. The war would claim two of his sons, Masami and Tetumi, but these deaths hardly affected their twin sisters, Eiko and Shizuko, who were just twelve when Pearl Harbor was attacked. Korea, though so close to Japan, was not engaged in the fighting and life for the twins was not all that bad. Eiko adored her sister, all the more so because Shizuko was shy and always rather sickly. In Eiko, the protective instinct was already strong and she seemed to possess everything her sister lacked: robust health and a tenacious character. She was not un-pretty either and made many friends among the boys and girls who played and swam at the Ginse beach near Seoul, where her father bought her ice-creams – a luxury the Koreans could not afford, any more than they could send their children to a school like Eiko's. Not that it mattered, for Eiko's school was in any case barred to Korean children.

School was fun for Eiko. The girls were told that Japan was always winning and that, even if the war front was so far away, it was their duty to help. This, Eiko did with a will; her personal contribution varied from mending soldiers' uniforms to working in the local fish factory, beating dried cod's roes with a wooden cudgel to extract the oil. Such was to be Eiko's war; she would never have to face its blatant horror – not, at least, until long after it was over.

4

Three days after the dramatic start of the Pacific war, two mighty British warships, *Prince of Wales*, pride of the Royal Navy, and the veteran battle cruiser *Repulse*, were patrolling in the gulf of Thailand when Japanese torpedo-bombers attacked them; both were sent to the bottom.

Germany's declaration of war against America was merely incidental in this trail of allied disaster – which was far from ended. Before Christmas the American islands of Guam and Wake, way out in the Pacific, were seized by the Japanese; the British stronghold, Hong Kong, fell on Christmas Day. Meanwhile the Japanese Army was sweeping down the Malayan peninsula towards Singapore; in the Philippines they had landed in the north of the main island, Luzon, and were pushing the Filipino-American forces southwards towards Bataan and Corregidor, across the bay from Manila.

In Japan, people were in a happy mood as they celebrated New Year's Day, the most popular holiday. The streets of Nagasaki, like those of every other town in Nippon, were thronged with crowds on their way to leave an offering at the family shrine. Oba-chan took the children to the great Suwa shrine down-town where the question on everybody's lips was: 'When shall we hear of the next victory?' They had not many weeks to wait. On 17 February 1942 the government triumphantly announced the capture of Singapore – the greatest disaster, according to Churchill, that ever befell British arms. Prime Minister Tojo, to mark the occasion, ordered a hand-out to every Japanese family of a bag of red beans, two bottles of beer and three *go* of sake. The children were not forgotten; Sumiteru, like all other under-thirteens, got a box of toffee and cakes.

As his history teacher explained to the class, the Pacific war, with the fall of Singapore, was now decided; Japan would go on winning until final victory. Less than two weeks later, there came yet another triumph when Japanese warships defeated an allied fleet in the Java Sea. By early March the island of Java, and with it the power and the wealth of oil and tin of the Netherlands' East Indies, was in the hands of the Japanese. Sumatra, Bali, Borneo and the Celebes were soon theirs too. Their troops were firmly lodged in New Guinea and plans were afoot to seize the whole island and press on eastwards, out-flanking Australia for the time being, on across the Coral Sea and out into the South Pacific as far as Fiji and Samoa.

In the West Pacific, the Japanese onslaught in the Philippines had cornered the Americans against the sea. At the beginning of April, after a brave but hopeless stand at Bataan, American and Filipino soldiers surrendered in their thousands. A month later, at Corregidor, thousands more were taken prisoner, many only to die at the hands of their captors during the 'Bataan death march' *en route* to their prison camps. Their Commander-in-Chief, General MacArthur, escaped at the last moment vowing, 'I shall return.'

In a few months the Japanese had ousted the Americans from the Philippines, the British from Burma, Malaya, Singapore and Hong Kong and the Dutch from the East Indies. Their grasp now extended across the Western Pacific, with the strategic island groups – the Marianas, the Carolines, the Marshalls, the Solomons and the Gilberts – all garrisoned by their troops.

Sumiteru and his school-mates were regaled with news of these astounding victories, but they never heard about the bestial treatment meted out by the victorious Japanese soldiers to their hundreds of thousands of prisoners.

One of them, leading aircraftsman Sidney Lawrence, an optician in civil life, had joined the RAF Volunteer Reserve. He was serving in 36 Torpedo Bomber Squadron at the fall of

Singapore. When the squadron was all but wiped out Lawrence was evacuated to Java in one of the three remaining Vickers Wildebeest aircraft, their tyres, for want of inner tubes, stuffed with grass. It was in Java, in March 1942, that he was captured by the Japanese.

The prisoners were lined up. A Japanese officer, escorted by two soldiers, asked the first prisoner in good English: 'Are you willing to work for Dai Nippon?' 'Not f . . . ing likely,' the RAF man replied. One of the soldiers knocked him senseless with his rifle butt, then finished him off on the ground. The officer moved to the next prisoner who was asked the same question; he gave the same answer and suffered the same fate. Lawrence, sixth in line, was praying, 'Dear God, give me courage not to be the first to go under,' when he heard the man next but one to him answer, 'I am willing to work for Dai Nippon.' When his turn came, Sid gave the same reply.

In October 1942, under the tropical sun, the prisoners, half starved and thirsting for water, were marched for several kilometres to Djakarta. One after another, men would stumble, on the point of collapse, then, supported by a comrade on each side, would struggle on. Some could find no more strength to continue; they fell by the roadside and were bayoneted where they lay.

A ship took the prisoners to Singapore where they were transferred to another vessel, the *Shonan Maru*. It had seen better days. A brass plate on the donkey engine was inscribed 'Made by Cammel Laird, Birkenhead, England'. The prisoners, some two thousand of them, were herded aboard. A day out from Singapore they were calling the *Shonan Maru* 'the hell ship'. Only 228 of them remained alive when it docked at Moji, in the north of Kyushu Island. In pouring rain and an icy wind they were still wearing tropical kit. More died after arrival, but Lawrence somehow managed to survive. More dead than alive he was put to work as a stevedore. When a German liner would put in to Moji, the jibes and laughter of the passengers did not even register on Lawrence and his fellow-prisoners, so exhausted were they.

Some time later Lawrence was transferred to a copper refinery further south – it reminded him of Dante's *Inferno*. Without realizing it, he was moving nearer to Nagasaki.

At the Asahi *shoga-ko* school in Nagasaki, Sumiteru, much as he disliked the ceaseless outpouring of bellicose propaganda, had no qualms about doing his bit for the war effort. Like all school-children, he had been conscripted into the civilian work-force before the war started. He had been put to work tunnelling air-raid shelters into the hillside and building roads which led up to anti-aircraft sites on the high ground. It was rugged work, wielding a pick-axe and carrying away the excavated mud and stones in a wicker basket, but Sumiteru, light-weight that he was, went about his job with a will. When war had broken out, everybody had to carry air-raid hoods, a first-aid kit and a label hung round their neck showing blood-type, name and address. Working hours were extended and school-children had to give up one-third of their school time to manual labour. It was asking a lot, but Sumiteru did not mind. The hill was preferable to the classroom and, besides, he felt content to be helping his country to speed the day of final victory.

Not that Sumiteru – or even his history teacher – realized how vital it was, if Japan were to be victorious, that the war should be a short one. So far it had been a whirlwind series of wins, but when, in May, the Japanese invasion fleet closed on Port Moresby, capital of New Guinea, it was intercepted in the Coral Sea by a strong force of American warships. The battle was fierce. The Japanese claimed victory, so did the Americans who from now on began to feel that the tide was on the turn.

Next month, June, in a risky attempt to seize Midway Island, which was closer to Pearl Harbor than Tokyo, the Japanese striking force once more met the American fleet and, this time, disaster. The Tokyo government, not least its Prime Minister, were badly shaken. 'Hide everything from the people,' ordered Tojo. So Sumiteru never heard that Japan, instead of forging ahead along the short road to victory, was now beginning a dismal journey down the long road to defeat.

34

It was Midway which decided the outcome of the war in the Pacific. In that vast area of sea, the Americans were beginning to roll back the enemy. Their first move was to seize the Japanese-held island of Guadalcanal, one of the Solomon Islands, beyond the eastern tip of New Guinea. The Japanese garrison offered little resistance to the first detachments of US marines who landed there in August, but reinforcements were rushed to the island, and in the narrow waters around it the opposing navies battled incessantly to keep the men on land supplied. On the island itself the carnage continued until, at the end of 1942, the last emaciated remnants of the Japanese defenders were overpowered.

Their defeat caused dismay among the war-lords in Tokyo. One of their angriest meetings degenerated into a drunken brawl, when insults were exchanged by service chiefs and even hurled at the Prime Minister. Each blamed the other for the failure to repulse the Americans from Guadalcanal. The army on the battlefield was blamed – unjustly, for surrender was forbidden to a Japanese soldier; like a cornered animal, he would resist until finally despatched, or use his last bullet, his last grenade, on himself. Stories of their soldiers' heroism reached the Japanese public. When Sumiteru heard them he became thoughtful; if ever he had to fight, he would have to try to fight like them, to the death.

The fighting qualities of the Japanese soldier moved General George Kenney, Chief of Allied Air Forces in the South West Pacific, to report: 'The Jap is still being underrated . . . We will have to call on all our patriotism, stamina, guts and maybe some crusading spirit or religious fervour thrown in, to beat him.' The future would prove him right. But neither he nor anyone, save a very few, suspected that there might be something very different to those human qualities, which would eventually be thrown in to beat the Japanese.

On 2 December 1942, in a top-secret experiment at the University of Chicago, Doctor Enrico Fermi, the Italian physicist, successfully demonstrated the world's first nuclear chain reaction – the key principle of the atomic bomb.

5

1943 for the Japanese, was the year of the sheep; during it, events were to determine the coming slaughter both on the battle-front and at home.

When they met at Casablanca in January, Roosevelt and Churchill agreed that, when the time came, as they were certain it would, Japan should be forced to accept unconditional surrender. In a similar mood, on the Pacific front, allied fighting men were out to avenge their comrades of the 'Bataan death march', the Burma Road and the gaols of Java. Increasingly, the fighting was to show contempt for human life. Atrocities were committed on both sides.

In Japan things were going badly wrong; the Navy was squabbling with the Air Force while the Army blamed them both for its own misfortunes, the latest of which was the recapture by America of Attic Island, a northern outpost in the Aleutians. The occupied territories – China, Burma, Malaya, and the East Indies – were not producing the expected quantities of raw materials and much of the produce shipped to Japan was being sunk *en route* by US submarines. The consequences were inevitable: production was falling and battle losses – ships, tanks and aircraft – were not being replaced. The Emperor was depressed, and when in June, a US fleet under Admiral Halsey put marines ashore on North Georgia, key to the Solomons, at huge cost to the Japanese, his confidence in the military fell to its lowest ebb. 'You keep on saying,' he complained to General Tojo, 'that the Army is invulnerable, yet whenever the enemy lands you lose the battle.' As Colonel Tanemura, the Cabinet diarist, noted: 'We are facing a very grave crisis.'

True as that was, it was not a crisis that directly affected Sumiteru. He had left school in March, just after his fourteenth birthday, and joined the post office as a postman – hardly the word, for he was so small that he could only just reach the pedals of his red post-office bicycle. His thighs became so chaffed that he had to ride most of the time standing on the pedals.

But Sumiteru had never been happier in his life, not least because, times being as hard as they were, he could now earn his own keep and pass on some of his wages to his grandmother, Oba-Chan. He was glad too that, while freed from the manual work on the hill, he was still working for the government. But what made him happiest was his new-found liberty; he was out all day in the open and often on the hill itself.

Sumiteru had passed on his dark blue school uniform, tunic trousers and cap to some new pupil and he now donned the khaki 'national uniform' of tunic, breeches and puttees. He wore a peaked cap, like a soldier's, and when necessary, a cape to protect him against cold and rain. His black mail-bag with its solid metal clasp was fastened to a carrier in front of his bicycle. A tyre repair kit was tucked into the saddlebag – punctures were an occupational hazard and had to be mended on the spot.

At first Sumiteru was puzzled by the addresses on the letters. Streets were neither named nor numbered and the address indicated only the registered number of the building and the *machi*, the district. A *machi* was divided into several *cho*, sub-districts. It needed a detective's flair to understand the system.

Sumiteru's base was the main post office opposite the city hall and the fire station in down-town Motohakata, and a few hundred metres down the street from the prefecture in neighbouring Edo-machi. The postmen took it in turn to operate four different services: normal letter deliveries, mail collection and special deliveries – the latter being allowed only for Mitsubishi and the *Kempetai* or special police; parcel deliveries and finally telegrams – these were delivered only to Mitsu-

37

bishi. The postman was given fifteen minutes to ride up-town to the Ordnance Factory; it was a challenge that Sumiteru enjoyed.

Again, the postmen took turns to work down-town and in the suburbs. When Sumiteru worked in the city he could get home for lunch, which Oba-chan had prepared for him. When he delivered in Nameshi-machi, the northeastern district up-town, she would make up a lunch-box for him, for it meant a longer day. At the end of it, tired out, he would leave his bicycle at the post office, then walk down past the prefecture to the Ohato pier, where he took the ferry – it had a screw each end to avoid turning round – to the Asahi-machi pier across the harbour. It took him another fifteen weary minutes to climb the path and the 150 steps up to his home. He was always glad to see Oba-chan and devour the meal she had cooked for him. For all the tricks he had used to play on his grandmother, the old lady had come to dote on him, especially now that Keiko and Teiji had left home to work in Osaka. She admired his pluck, and his high spirits encouraged her in these times of shortage and rationing.

For his part, Sumiteru loved his job; he soon became a familiar figure at the houses and shops where he called, and with the children playing in the streets. While he took his duties seriously, they gave him scope for adventure and challenged his endurance, as the hill had always done and still did. When the gradient became too steep for pedalling, he would sling his bicycle on one shoulder and climb on foot to deliver to the houses at the top. Then he would jump on the saddle and hurtle back down the hill, taking the steps in his stride. When returning from up-town he would race down beside the railway line, keeping pace with the train, until it came to the next stop. Then he would shove his bicycle aboard, jump in after it and take a free ride down to the terminus. At the upper limit of his territory, the Urakami dam, then under construction, the road ran out and Sumiteru had to lower his bicycle on the end of a rope to the bottom of a ravine, wade through water and climb up, humping the machine to where the road began again.

Sumiteru loved his red bicycle, most of all for the wild sensation of speed that it gave him. He had to pedal for his life when a couple of sheep dogs belonging to the blacksmith near the Ohashi stadium, tore after him. He outstripped them and was triumphant. Sometimes he rode so fast that he felt as if he were flying. His thrill for speed knew no bounds until the day he crashed headlong into the muddy water of a paddy field. The red bicycle and its rider, covered with grime, did not escape the notice of Sumiteru's chief, who gave the boy a sound ticking-off. Sumiteru's friend Honda met a more painful fate: racing along the bank of the Urakami, he skidded into the river and broke four teeth. His own and Honda's mishaps made Sumiteru more careful in future, for he wanted to keep his job. Combining as it did serious duty with excitement he could not dream of a better one. Life was never so good and the war seemed far away.

In fact, it was moving inexorably closer. Following the seizure in June of North Georgia by the US Navy and marines, it was Admiral Nimitz's task force that landed more marines on the Gilberts, the most easterly of Japan's Pacific outposts. By November the islands were in US hands and Tojo was beginning to wonder where to establish his last line of defence.

On the allied political front, Stalin, meeting with Roosevelt and Churchill at Teheran in the same month, promised them that, once Germany was defeated, the Soviets would join America and Britain in the war against Japan. One night after a late session, Churchill, as he went to bed, was struck by the gloomy thought that man might destroy man and wipe out civilization. He knew all about the American nuclear bomb project, code-named 'Manhattan', for Britain was making an important contribution both in know-how and scientists. Fermi's successful experiment in nuclear fission was now nearly a year old.

With the Gilberts secured, Nimitz's task force, early in the new year of 1944, turned north and set course for the Marshall Islands. Taken by surprise the Japanese garrisons on the atolls of Kwajalein and Eniwetok were overwhelmed. Nimitz then steered west towards the Carolines where Truk, the base of the Japanese Combined Fleet's warships and aircraft, was heavily bombarded – yet another disaster for Japanese arms.

Tojo was blamed; never had he been so unpopular with the *jushin*, the 'club' of ex-Prime Ministers, who wanted him to be removed forthwith and replaced by a Prime Minister who would immediately sue for peace. The Emperor's senior advisers already knew that Japan's defeat was inevitable. The analysis made by the brilliant strategist, Admiral Takagi, of the catastrophic losses in shipping and aircraft, confirmed their view. 'Japan cannot win the war,' he said, adding that the only solution was Tojo's dismissal; the Admiral was actually plotting to assassinate him. One way or another, he recommended that Tojo's departure should be followed by an overture for peace, whatever the consequences. This was early in 1944.

Tojo did not budge. As the American fleet veered north from the Carolines towards the Mariana Islands – Saipan, Tinian and Guam – the Japanese Premier gave his personal promise to guarantee their defence.

The Marianas were Nimitz's coveted prize, the most strategic islands in the Pacific. Air bases there would enable US bombers to attack Japan directly.

In mid-June US marines landed on Saipan. The Japanese Mobile Fleet moved in, but was intercepted by Admiral Spruance's aircraft carrier and routed with disastrous losses. The action, called the Battle of the Philippines Sea and nicknamed (by the victorious US Navy fliers) the 'Marianas turkey shoot', marked, according to one Japanese observer, the end of the Japanese Combined Fleet, and of Japan.

As the battle on Saipan Island raged, Tokyo signalled General Iseta, commanding the Japanese garrison: 'Continue to destroy the enemy and thus assuage the Emperor's anxiety,' to which the General replied, 'We hope to requite the imperial favour.' But this the Japanese soldiers failed to do, despite their fanatical resistance which cost the destruction of almost their entire garrison of 22,000 men. The Americans, too, paid dearly, with 14,000 men killed, missing and wounded. But by July 1944, Saipan was theirs and, soon after, Tinian and Guam. A rain of steel and fire and of a horror yet unknown, could now be delivered by US bombers against the Japanese mainland.

In Tokyo, the Army General Staff reported: 'There is now no hope for Japan to reverse the unfavourable war situation . . . It is time for us to end the war.' Tojo was forced to resign and General Koiso, the 'Tiger of Korea', became Prime Minister.

While the Americans were subduing Saipan, another American force, an immense armada of ships carrying 165,000 troops, with General MacArthur in command, was sailing towards the Philippines. One of the central islands, Leyte, was their first objective. As US marines began landing there, three separate Japanese fleets, including aircraft carriers, converged on Leyte with the urgent task of destroying the enemy transports lying off-shore. But the Japanese received such a fearful trouncing from the US fleet that the Imperial Navy was never again able to take any useful part in the defence of the homeland. Their Air Force, too, was permanently crippled.

MacArthur's men still had to fight hard to recapture the main island of Luzon. Bataan and Corregidor were retaken in January 1945 and MacArthur's vow, 'I shall return', was fulfilled. By March, Manila was in American hands – but not the American prisoners of war held there. They had been shipped to Japan; of some four thousand, only six hundred survived the voyage. Stories of their terrible sufferings, of the atrocities perpetrated by the Japanese against the civil population of Manila – all that added to memories of the 'Bataan death march' – subdued any feeling of pity that Americans at the front and at home might have had for the Japanese enemy.

With the Philippines once more in their hands, the Americans had but two island fortresses, Iwo Jima and Okinawa, between them and the Japanese homeland. By February, a desperate battle for Iwo Jima was already engaged.

While the truth about Japan's disastrous situation on the battle-front could be concealed from the public, there had recently been growing signs of the worst calamity of all – air raids on the homeland itself – strategic air-raids intended to destroy Japanese industry. B.29 Super-fortresses of the Very Long Range – VLR – bomber force, operating from bases in non-Japanese-occupied China, had been making sporadic attacks on Tokyo and other cities since July 1944. The 'Bees', as the public nicknamed them, were visible to every Japanese; the crash of their bombs, day and night, could not be silenced. Nagasaki had so far been spared. Sumiteru, however urgent his mission, could never resist the temptation to stop in his tracks and gaze up at the marvellous sight of the bombers, ten kilometres overhead, glinting like silver fish and streaming white vapour trails across the sky, on their way to bomb targets further north. But while these raids certainly impressed the public, they did little damage to Japanese war industry.

Since the capture of the Mariana Islands, better bases, closer to the target, became available to the US bomber force. By November 1944 they were ready to strike. But showers of high explosives from hundreds of Bees, while they sent people running to the shelters, still failed to make any serious impact on Japanese military targets. Then Nagoya, Japan's third largest city, which had just been smitten by an earthquake, was lambasted by high explosive bombs. What a pitiful contrast this raid provided to man at his best, in peace-time, when aircraft would have flown in on life-saving missions carrying food and medicine. The raid on Nagoya was perhaps an even more callous episode than any other in the process which, since Guernica, had been degrading mankind: the bombing of defenceless civilians from the air.

Yet General Curtis Le May, the commander of the US bomber force in the Marianas, was not content; his offensive was not achieving its objective of destroying Japanese war industry, two-thirds of which was dispersed in private homes and small workshops. High explosive bombs were effective enough against precise targets but not against these thousands of small scattered industrial plants. Le May hit on what he called a radical plan; he would burn them out, wholesale. He ordered his B.29s to be stripped of all guns except the rear turret, as well as of all superfluous equipment, and to be loaded to capacity with bombs filled with napalm, jellied fuel which ignited on impact – the most deadly of all incendiary devices.

Well aware as he was that his new tactics would cause massive slaughter of civilians, Le May despatched, on the night of 9 March, over 300 B.29s. Their orders were to set fire to the heart of Tokyo, where, in houses made of wood and paper, there lived, until that awful night, a quarter of a million low-paid workers. By dawn, 130,000 of them with their families lay strewn about the city in heaps of charred, unrecognizable corpses. During the nights that followed, B.29s burnt to death thousands more civilians in Nagoya, Kobe and Osaka.

The bombing war was escalating to its peak. As the Germans had rained fire on British cities, as the British and Americans had in turn done worse to the Germans, so now the Americans were meting out worse still to the Japanese. Their fire-raising attacks on Japanese cities, far from showing concern for the lives of non-combatants, were aimed directly at them. And this was only the beginning of the holocaust.

The battle for Iwo Jima, begun in February, was now reaching its bloody climax. The Japanese, refusing to surrender, were being burnt out of their bunkers and foxholes by flame-throwers. 'The gods would weep at the bravery of my men,' was the last message of their commander, General Kuribayashi. Next day, he committed *hara-kiri*. Sumiteru was always moved when he read in the papers of the fanatical resistance of those simple soldiers.

The battle for Iwo Jima had cost five thousand American lives, seventeen thousand Japanese – small figures compared with the numbers of Japanese civilians dying in air-raids at home.

It was the end of March and 185,000 American troops were

waiting in transports off Okinawa, ready to assault this last bastion between them and the Japanese homeland. As Japanese citizens continued to perish in the flames of the B.29s' napalm, Prince Konoye, one-time Prime Minister, warned the Emperor: 'Japan has lost the war.' But, he added, the Army, though they knew they were beaten, would do everything to deny peace. They intended to drag the nation into a last suicidal fight to the death, a national *hara-kiri*. 'One hundred million will die together', was their slogan. Prime Minister Koiso had exhorted the nation: 'Now is the time for us, the one hundred million, to give vent to our flaming ardour and follow the valiant men of the Special Attack Corps – the *Kami-kaze*.' These suicide pilots were causing some havoc among the American ships lying off Okinawa, but they were unable to daunt the valour or resist the crushing weight of the American assault. By early April the Japanese Army Chief of Staff, General Umezu, admitted, 'The battle for Okinawa is going badly.' Koiso resigned and seventy-eight-year-old Admiral Suzuki resumed the premiership, promising to implement the Emperor's desire, to end the war as soon as possible.

With things going so badly for the Japanese at Okinawa, the remnants of the Second Fleet – ten ships including the super-dreadnaught *Yamato* ('Japan') – were despatched to the island. It was a suicide mission, everyone concerned knew, without air cover: long before the Japanese fleet reached Okinawa it was attacked by US Navy planes. Two ships survived, but the *Yamato* was not one of them. Hit by twelve torpedoes, 'Japan', pride of the Imperial Navy, capsized and sank. A more convincing symbol could not have been provided of the country's own plight.

A week later, on 12 April, President Roosevelt died suddenly. In Germany, Nazi leaders tried to convince the nation, now on the verge of defeat, that the President's disappearance was a last-minute deliverance. The Japanese were not so foolish; the battle for Okinawa had reached a stage of unspeakable savagery. Japanese soldiers, joined by thousands of Okinawan students, were being slaughtered without quarter by American armour and scorched by flame-throwers, while in the air, *Kami-kaze* pilots, pledged to die a meaningful death, relentlessly pressed home their attacks on American ships.

6

Over the homeland, B.29s by hundreds kept up their strategic round-the-clock fire-raids. Feeble though the Japanese fighter and anti-aircraft defences were, the bomber crews, as they approached the target, would slip on their armoured 'flak-suits'. The 'bomber boys' were likened to mediaeval knights going into battle, but in reality they were nothing of the sort. Among the knights of old there existed a code of chivalry which, if it was not always respected, at least served as a standard by which their conduct might be judged. The crews of the strategic bombers, with industry and public morale as their targets, could not allow themselves to be moved by any such spirit of mercy towards the weak and the defenceless, as the code of chivalry demanded. Flying in the face of enemy defences, of the hazards of weather and technical failure, they were men of rare courage. But all comparison between them and the knights in armour ended there. Though the courage of the bomber crews might have been exemplary, they were the antithesis of the 'verray parfit gentil knight'.

Their ultimate criterion was technical competence – to achieve the greatest destruction. Each member of the crew was a highly specialized practitioner in his particular trade: pilot, navigator, weaponer, bombardier, radio and radar operator, air gunner, men equipped with sophisticated electronic devices, heavily armed with steel and fire and explosive, who unleashed their weapons not against other men similarly armed, but against the defenceless population. The greatest casualties in the air war had been not airmen, but non-combatants – men, women and children on the ground below.

The air, if it had inspired man to some of his most heroic exploits, had debased him also to his most inhuman.

Americans at home (who had never been bombed in their lives) would say, 'The Japs deserve every bomb dropped on them.' The men in power – on both sides – saw the civilian population as an anonymous, expendable mass whose function was to face the enemy, unarmed and inadequately protected, and submit to the slaughter.

The sufferings of the Japanese people were far from ended. A new explosive device, deadly secret and referred to by those in the know as the 'special bomb', was in the offing.

By June, with Japan's greatest cities laid waste by fire, Okinawa was firmly in American hands. The comparative losses were staggering. The battle had cost the lives of 12,500 GIs, US marines and navy men; 200,000 Japanese soldiers and students had vainly sacrificed their own lives to defend the island – a crushing defeat for Japan in the last battle outside the homeland.

Yet the Japanese Cabinet, to the Emperor's profound dismay, now adopted a new resolution: to continue the war. The public was told that every man, woman and child was to be prepared to die in a last stand on the mainland. In the prisoner-of-war camps throughout the country, allied prisoners were paraded before the commandant, who informed them that invasion was imminent. As soon as the enemy set foot on Japanese soil, all prisoners of war would be put to death. They were even told how: by machine-guns, flame-throwers or by being sealed into caves which would then be blown in by explosives. For this sinister purpose prisoners in No. 14 Fukuoka camp in Nagasaki were put to work digging out tunnels in the hillside. One of those unfortunate men was Sid Lawrence. He had just been transferred to the camp.

The last-ditch operation was named *Ketsu-go*, the decision for the suicidal defence of the homeland. Available for the purpose were ten thousand aircraft (many of them trainers), two and a half million regular troops, four million army and navy employees, plus a voluntary militia of twenty-eight million. The spirit was admirable; it recalled Churchill's exhortation in 1940 to the British to fight the Germans on the beaches and in the hills. But Britain then had her empire, and America, though not yet at war, was known to be behind her. For Japan, without a fighting friend in the world, was *Ketsu-go* feasible?

Already in May, a government investigation had shown that Japan's shortages were far more critical than realized. There was a desperate lack of raw materials – most of the plunder despatched from the conquered countries lay at the bottom of the sea; half of the Japanese merchant navy had been sunk, not to mention its fighting navy which was now virtually non-existent. Munitions' production had dropped to two-thirds below normal. Within weeks, said the report, there would be no more inter-city trains, no more steel ships; the chemical industry, too, was on the verge of collapse. Reserves of the most basic and vital of all commodities – oil – were fast running out; attempts to refine aviation fuel from the resin of pine trees produced only a derisory three thousand barrels. Finally, the rice crop had failed; the daily food ration had fallen below five hundred calories and acorns were on the daily menu.

Shocked by the report, the inner cabinet, the Big Six, discussed for the first time on 12 May a plan to negotiate peace through Russia. An envoy, Sato, would be sent to Moscow; his mission, though Tokyo could not know it, was doomed from the start, for Stalin, months before, had promised to join the Allies in the war against Japan once Germany was beaten. Germany had surrendered four days earlier, on 8 May.

Privately, Japanese civilian ministers, opposed to the fanatical military, were expressing fears that the food shortage, coupled with the unceasing fire-raids, would lead to public unrest or, worse, a protest movement against the Emperor, whom some were already blaming for continuing the war. Traditionally, however, the Emperor, constitutional monarch as he was, could not intervene on the political scene, though he was deeply aware and acutely sensitive to it, thanks to his personal adviser, the Privy Seal, Marquis Kido, a sage and reasonable man. Kido, like Konoye, and many others, was so profoundly disturbed by events that he made out a long report for the Emperor in which he concluded that, whatever happened, Japan could not possibly wage war beyond the end of 1945 at the latest. 'Japan must end hostilities,' he advised the Emperor, and begged His Majesty to intervene, exceptionally, unconstitutionally, and personally to sue for peace.

The Emperor was willing. Addressing the Big Six at the end of June, he reminded them of their recent resolution to continue the war, to fight a last, suicidal battle in defence of the homeland. Since then, he told them, he had come to favour another policy. 'I deem it necessary,' he told his senior ministers, 'to consider a move for peace'; and he bade them put his wishes into effect. Negotiations through Moscow were to be pressed forward.

Japan, everyone present knew, was a defeated nation. But the *gumbatsu*, the military clique, while professing abject respect for their imperial master, were not inclined to obey his wishes. They believed that, if they could bring the enemy to battle on Japanese soil, they would inflict on him such heavy losses that they could then sue for an honourable peace. Kido, Konoye and others knew better: how were those ten thousand *Kami-kaze* planes to leave the ground without aviation fuel or their pilots to die a meaningful death without bombs? And how were the tanks and infantry, short of ammunition, to vie with an enemy possessing a crushing weight of fire power on land, on the sea and in the air? What stomach would the twenty-eight million-strong militia have for battle on a starvation diet and armed only with muzzle-loading rifles, bows and arrows, bamboo spears for the schoolgirls and daggers for the boys? Sumiteru, as he handled his own bamboo dagger, wondered how he could ever emulate the heroic defenders of Iwo Jima and Okinawa.

7

While in Tokyo the Cabinet groped hesitatingly for an honourable peace, while in Moscow envoy Sato tried, with no success, to get Russia to mediate, developments of sinister portent for Japan were preparing in Washington. Upon the decisions taken in those three cities, the fate of countless multitudes and of one young boy, Sumiteru, would depend.

Harry Truman, former US Vice-President and the man who had automatically succeeded Roosevelt, was relatively insignificant compared with his illustrious predecessor. Brought up on a farm in Missouri, Truman soon developed a passion for history. He had read the Bible three times over. After serving without distinction as an artilleryman at the end of World War I, he was demobilized and went into business. He set up a store in Kansas City selling haberdashery and ready-to-wear. But times were hard and Harry Truman was soon bankrupt. He then entered local politics, little dreaming that his career, with its modest beginnings, would lead him to the presidency of the United States.

Until he succeeded Roosevelt, Truman had never heard – so closely guarded a secret was it – of the Manhattan project, let alone the 'special bomb'. An 'Interim Committee', presided over by the Secretary for War Harold Stimson, was set up to advise him. It included a number of civilians as well as some nuclear scientists. In June 1945, while Emperor Hirohito was urging his ministers to seek peace with all speed, the Interim Committee was deliberating the use of the atomic bomb, two of which would soon be ready. Stimson, briefed by Robert Oppenheimer, the brilliant scientist who had designed and constructed the bomb, was appalled by the destructive effect it would have on human life. He insisted it be used to destroy military targets, not human lives. His sentiments were noble, but pathetically naive, for most strategic 'military', that is industrial, targets were situated in densely populated areas. Despite Stimson's misgivings, the Committee decided that the bomb should be used as soon as possible – and without warning – against 'such a target as to make clear its devastating strength'. The minutes of one of its meetings recorded: '. . . we could not concentrate on a civilian area; but that we should seek to make a profound psychological impression on as many inhabitants as possible . . . the most desirable target would be a vital war plant employing a large number of workers and closely surrounded by workers' houses.' Those committee men were disingenuous in suggesting that the atomic bomb would cause just a 'psychological impression' on the inhabitants. And even though they might argue that civilian factory workers were 'combatants' and therefore fit to be killed, they must also have realized that the bomb's 'devastating strength' would ensure the wholesale massacre of their families living in the houses which 'closely surrounded' the factory.

Truman himself insisted that the bomb be used against a military target. He wanted, he said, to make sure that the weapon would be used as a weapon of war, in a manner prescribed by the laws of war – whose object, among others, was the protection of non-combatants. Truman's thinking was, at best, muddled, at worst dishonest.

The multitudes of civilians killed during air-raids against 'military targets' in Europe and Japan were evidence enough for the President to understand that there was no such thing as bombing an industrial target and at the same time sparing the lives of non-combatants. Moreover, since the R.A.F. had decided in 1942 that the German public's morale was a legitimate target and had adopted 'area bombing' – the saturation with high explosive and incendiary bombs of a wide area surrounding the target – the Americans had imitated the technique. It was now accepted policy to make war, by bombing non-combatants. The pious concern of the President and his advisers for the laws of war and the welfare of civilians was bunk. They knew perfectly well that, however 'military' the weapon and the target, massive execution of non-combatants was inevitable and often intentional.

Doctor Franck, a Nobel prize winner, and seven other scientists working on the Manhattan project were more forth-right. They begged the Interim Committee to contrive first a non-military demonstration of the atomic bomb so that the Japanese could realize its devastating strength. The scientists argued that, if America were to use this unprecedented means of destruction, it would be held responsible for the consequences. But Doctor Franck and his colleagues never mentioned the most terrible consequence of all – radioactivity. The explosion of both 'conventional' and nuclear weapons caused fire and blast, but only nuclear weapons emit radioactive rays and particles whose malignant effects may persist in nature and mankind for generations. This scientific fact was known to Doctor Franck and his colleagues. Even more than the weapon's 'devastating strength', it was the best argument against using the atomic bomb. But the scientists failed to expose this to the Committee, who rejected the rest of their arguments.

One means open to the Americans of securing Japan's ultimate surrender was invasion. The US Chief of Staff, General Marshall, believed it might cost over half a million American lives; the invasion, if it were to be, would not be launched until September at the earliest. Stimson's committee, while not eliminating invasion as a possibility, concluded that the atom bomb was a preferable alternative – that is, if Japan did not accept unconditional surrender.

The Emperor, as he had already instructed his inner cabinet, had every intention of surrendering. But a problem bothered the Cabinet: they feared that surrender would mean the end of their emperor-system, of the *Kokutai*, the national essence, which stemmed from the legend that the Japanese Emperor, who had reigned from time immemorial, would go on reigning for ever. His elimination would mean the death of the Japanese nation.

With his forty-five years' experience as a politician and statesman Churchill, for one, had suggested to Truman that this be borne in mind. But the most authentic, convincing plea came from Joseph Grew, for ten years US ambassador in Tokyo, who understood better than any westerner the Japanese in the depths of their oriental minds. In a private meeting with Truman he advised the President to issue a proclamation to the Japanese Government stating that unconditional surrender did not mean the end of the imperial system.

Many of Truman's senior advisers supported Grew; they included Stimson, Forrestal, the Navy Secretary, and General Marshall, preoccupied as he was with planning the invasion of Japan. Admiral Leahy, with his long experience of war, diplomacy and politics, thought that the demand for unconditional surrender would only make the Japanese resist more fiercely. Stimson's Assistant War Secretary, John McCloy, told Truman to his face: 'We should have our heads examined if we don't consider a political solution.' McCloy suggested sending a message to the Emperor demanding unconditional surrender with the assurance that the imperial regime would remain. A draft declaration was prepared; it included a clause which said 'This [the future Japanese Government] may include a constitutional monarchy under the present dynasty.' Truman gave his approval and left for Potsdam, near Berlin, there to confer with Churchill and Stalin. On the way, he changed his mind and eliminated the vital clause. In so doing, Truman made the dropping of the atomic bomb a certainty – as indeed he had always intended.

The President had never hidden his enthusiasm for the bomb; if it could be built, it could be used and he never doubted that it would be. By the time he left for Potsdam two were ready. On 16 July, the day after his arrival in Germany, a message from Stimson informed him that a trial atomic bomb, charged with plutonium, had been successfully exploded at Alamagordo, New Mexico.

During the next ten days, things moved fast. Stimson, on arriving in Potsdam, found, in his own words, that Truman was 'tremendously pepped up'. Churchill noticed that he told the Russians where they got off and generally tried to dominate the whole meeting. It was natural. The former bankrupt haberdasher from Kansas City, with the atom bomb in his pocket, was now the most powerful man on earth.

Truman was set on using the atom bomb; Churchill agreed, despite his gloomy visions of mankind destroying itself. Stalin was left in the dark; Truman merely told him that the Americans had a new weapon of unusual destructive force.

Truman's military advisers were deeply worried. General 'Hap' Arnold, chief of the US Army Air Forces, was convinced, in the light of the destruction wrought on Japanese cities up to date, that 'conventional' bombing alone could end the war. General Eisenhower, Commander-in-Chief of the victorious allied armies which had beaten the Germans into surrender in Europe, insisted that Japan also was already defeated. The atom bomb, in his opinion, was unnecessary and was no longer, as he put it, 'mandatory as a measure to save American lives'. Admiral Leahy thought that those concerned in the nuclear programme only wanted to use the bomb because of the vast sums of money – two billion dollars – spent on it. Foremost among the latter was the Manhattan project's ambitious director, General Groves; for him there was no question but that the bomb must be used. As he bluntly remarked, 'The war's over as soon as we drop one or two on Japan.' Subsequent events were to prove that it would need more than that to end the war.

Many of the scientists involved were having second thoughts. Doctor Leo Szilard, virtually the initiator, with Albert Einstein's support, of the atom-bomb project, and fifty-seven of his colleagues from Chicago (where nuclear fission had first been achieved), were frightened by the monster they had created; they now demanded that Japan should be warned and given the chance to surrender. They were too late. Truman had already decided – 'like that,' he told someone, snapping his fingers. With that trite gesture he condemned hundreds of thousands of innocent Japanese to death and life-long suffering. Young Sumiteru was to be one of the President's victims.

On 25 July, Truman had orders sent to 509 Composite Group, on Tinian Island in the Marianas, to drop their one available uranium bomb as soon as possible after 3 August. That same day the allied surrender ultimatum – the Potsdam Proclamation – was beamed to Japan. It warned the Japanese of the utter devastation of their cities that would follow if they did not surrender. Though the ultimatum reassured them that the Japanese nation would not be enslaved or destroyed, it did not contain a promise to keep the Emperor.

Not surprisingly, Tokyo rejected the Potsdam Proclamation out of hand; the Japanese press treated it with derision. A nuclear attack on Japan was now inevitable. Truman and his advisers had chosen the targets – they were designated as 'cities'. First on the list was Hiroshima, the reason being that it was an important army base – it was indeed the headquarters of the 2nd Army, but military personnel represented only a small percentage of the remaining civilian population of some 250,000 souls (luckily, considerable numbers had been evacuated). Other cities chosen for eventual extinction were Kokura, Niigata and Nagasaki.

At Tinian Island, in the early hours of 6 August, the base chaplain blessed the eleven-man crew, captained by Colonel Paul Tibbets, of the B.29 bomber. 'May the men who fly this night be kept safe,' he prayed, but breathed not a word of compassion for their tens of thousands of intended victims. At 2.45 local time, the B.29, with its four-ton atom bomb, climbed away from Tinian. On the bomber's side was painted the name of 'Enola Gay' – Colonel Tibbets' mother. As he steered his bomber northwards towards the site of the massacre, Tibbets puffed away at his pipe. 'There's something relaxing,' he remarked, 'in surrounding yourself with the smoke from an aromatic tobacco.'

Enola Gay was over Hiroshima at about 8 a.m. local time, unmolested either by flak or fighters. The bombardier, Major Thomas Ferebee, aimed not at the target, 2nd Army headquarters, but a more prominent landmark, the T-shaped Aioi bridge. No matter; no matter either if the atom bomb missed the aiming point – which it did, by three hundred metres. It's 'devastating strength' obliterated the entire city and nearly half of its inhabitants, an atrocity with which Colonel Tibbets had chosen, surprisingly, to associate his mother.

As Enola Gay turned for home, the crew cheered; Tibbets lit up his pipe once more and its blue smoke drifted across the flight deck. Behind him a column of purplish black smoke, mushroom-shaped at the top, rose up several kilometres above Hiroshima. All that remained of the city was a smouldering waste-land upon which rain soon began to fall, no ordinary rain, but heavy drops, black and greasy – 'black rain' precipitated from the atomic cloud and full of radioactive particles.

The news of Hiroshima was flashed to Truman aboard the USS *Augusta*, now on its way back to America. 'This is the greatest thing in history,' he exclaimed, an observation which hardly supported his claim to be an authority on history.

Back in Washington, he announced his intention of dropping another A-bomb – or two, or more – on the Japanese. He would give them three days to surrender – it could have been a few more, but for the fact that the deteriorating weather over Japan threatened to rob him of the chance of launching a second attack against Japanese cities. Two men who, in their long lives, had learnt far more than Truman about human nature, tried to dissuade him. Stimson told him, 'When you punish your dog you don't keep souring him after the punishment is over.' The Japanese, he added, were naturally a smiling people and the President should try to get on those terms with them. Old Admiral Leahy was more pointed. He told the President that he would be using an inhuman weapon on a defeated people. Truman's – and the American public's – standards, he said, were common to the barbarians of the Dark Ages.

Neither of these wise counsellors succeeded in staying Truman's hand. He would demonstrate to the Japanese – and the Russians too – his own and America's might. So sure was he of himself that he was foolish enough to predict: 'Never will the Russians have the atomic bomb.' Yet the day after Hiroshima, Stalin gave urgent orders to build one. It would take four years, but the armaments race was already on.

Before he ordered the bombing of Hiroshima, Truman was well aware that any day now the Russians would declare war on Japan. He could have waited, before immolating Hiroshima, to assess the effect of the imminent Russian invasion of Manchuria. Now that Hiroshima had been wiped out, Truman would still have had time to judge the effect of both Hiroshima and the Russian offensive. A possible US invasion of Japan was not scheduled until more than three weeks later. But Truman gave the Japanese only three days to capitulate. During that time, he ordered the Navy and the Air Force to 'keep up the pressure' by attacking with conventional bombs. Nagasaki was among the many cities hit on 8 August. The Mitsubishi steel works, the Inasa cemetery and the harbour installations were damaged. Sumiteru was home for lunch that day, it was his turn for night duty: from the house, he watched as an American bomber – it was smaller than a B.29 – dived on Dejima Quay. Its bombs made a huge splash, then the bomber zoomed up, passing so low over the house that Sumiteru could see the pilot. It was a thrilling sight – seen from a safe distance.

The 8 August was a day was full of action. American aircraft dropped millions of leaflets on Japanese cities. Their message was plain: the Americans had destroyed Hiroshima with one atomic bomb, the most destructive explosive devised by man. It went on: 'Before using this bomb to destroy every resource of the military by which they are prolonging this useless war we ask you now to petition the Emperor to end the war . . . Otherwise we shall resolutely employ this bomb.'

'Before using this bomb . . . petition the Emperor . . . otherwise we shall resolutely employ this bomb.' The wording was as deceptive as could be, for the next bomb was virtually already on the way. That same afternoon, on Tinian Island, Major Charles (Chuck) Sweeney had received orders to drop 'the next bomb' – next day. That evening, in Moscow, the Japanese envoy Sato was informed by Molotov, Soviet Foreign Minister, that as from midnight on 8 August, Russia would be at war with Japan.

It was the Russian invasion of Manchuria, begun well before midnight on the 8th, that clinched the Japanese decision to surrender. It dashed all their hopes of a negotiated peace. Prime Minister Suzuki's immediate reaction on hearing of the Russian invasion was: 'Let us end the war.' He found the Emperor agreeable to accept any terms; Hirohito had already remarked, on hearing of Hiroshima, 'We must put an end to the war. This tragedy must not be repeated.'

But now it was too late. Truman had already ordered a second atom-bomb attack. The primary target was defined as 'Kokura arsenal and city' – Kokura was part of a huge agglomeration on the north of Kyushu Island. The secondary target, in the south of the island, was designated 'Nagasaki urban area'. Truman's advisory committee had decided in June: 'We could not concentrate on a civilian area.' What other than a civilian area could Kokura 'city' and Nagasaki 'urban area' be?

8

The Japanese inner cabinet, the Big Six, had been summoned to an emergency meeting on the morning of 9 August, to hear Suzuki announce his intention of accepting unconditional surrender. It was 11 a.m. At that very moment, Sweeney's B.29, having been thwarted by clouds over Kokura, was starting its bombing run on the secondary target, Nagasaki.

The aircraft, named Bock's Car after Captain Frederick Bock Jr. who usually flew it, had taken off from Tinian just before 4 a.m. (3 a.m. Japanese time). Hardly had it settled on course than there was trouble with the fuel circuit, but Sweeney pressed on north towards the primary target, Kokura. He found the city obscured by smoke and haze. Bombardier Kermit Beahan had orders to make a visual drop, but on each of the aircraft's three runs over the city he had to report to the captain on the intercom: 'I can't pick up the aiming point.' Those few, frustrated words meant that Kokura was spared, Nagasaki condemned.

With the fuel supply now getting critical, Sweeney swung the Superfortress south towards Nagasaki, eighty kilometres away, only to find, as he neared the city, that it too was covered by a layer of nine-tenths cloud. The aiming point was downtown, between the main post office and the prefecture, on the rising ground above the port. A hit there would wipe out the port and the Mitsubishi shipyard opposite and reach up to the factories in the valley.

Badly worried by the fuel shortage, Sweeney told navy commander Ashworth, the weaponer – it was he who was in charge of the bomb – 'I can only make one run.' If the aiming point could not be identified visually, Ashworth had orders to jettison the bomb over the sea. What a waste, he thought. The 200,000 people below in Nagasaki would have disagreed, but it was the young naval commander alone who at this moment held power of life and death over them. He decided to disobey orders. Nagasaki was on the radar-scope. 'Go ahead then and bomb by radar,' he shouted to Sweeney.

It was 11 a.m. local time. Beahan, peering down, suddenly cried out, 'I can see the city.' But he could only see part of it; the down-town area where the aiming point lay was hidden by cloud. Beahan had his sights on an oval stadium; it was the Ohashi stadium where Sumiteru had once been chased by the blacksmith's dogs, on the left bank of the Urakami river, three kilometres up the valley from the intended aiming point. 'It will have to do,' the bombardier decided. The bomb would devastate the whole of Nagasaki, anyway. He pressed the release and Sweeney, to escape the blast, banked Bock's Car into a dive away from the city. The bomb fell free for about forty seconds; the burst-point ('epicentre') had been pre-set at a height of some five hundred metres above ground level. The maximum force of the explosion was concentrated at a point on the ground directly below (the 'hypocentre'). It was two hundred metres away from Beahan's aiming point and in the heart of Urakami district. No district in Nagasaki could have answered better to the target definition. With its private houses, its schools and hospitals, its university, temples and cathedral, its parks and peaceful tree-lined streets, Urakami district was the very model of an urban area. Out of its midst, there burst a giant ball of fire, hotter than the sun, belching smoke, and towering skywards for five kilometres in a dense orange-black column from the top of which there issued a heaving mass of cloud, mushroom-shaped and seething with radioactive dust and vapour. Somewhere at the foot of that column lay Sumiteru.

When Bock's Car had taken off from Tinian, Sumiteru was stretched out on a *tatami*, fast asleep, on the floor of the main post office. During the last few days, with the increasing air-raids, he had been on night duty helping to evacuate post office records and doing his stint of fire-watching. In the early hours of the 9th he managed to snatch some sleep.

Shortly after 7.30, when he woke up, Oba-chan came with two lunch-boxes. They chatted for a while, then Sumiteru told his grandmother: 'Now you must hurry back home; there may be another air-raid today.' As soon as she was gone, Sumiteru opened the lunch-boxes, first one, then the other. So hungry was he that he emptied them both.

At just on nine o'clock, he left the post office on his red bicycle with his friend Honda who had to deliver that day in the outer suburbs. It was a glorious morning, very warm, without a cloud in the sky, but Sumiteru, clad in breeches and puttees, striped blue and white short-sleeved shirt and uniform cap, enjoyed the rush of cool air as he sped down the hill with Honda towards Route 206. The two boys parted when they reached the Nishi (West) Urakami district. While Honda pedalled on up Route 206 towards the suburbs at the top of the valley, Sumiteru began his deliveries. He was only a hundred metres or so from the sub-office in Sumiyoshi-cho when his back tyre went flat. It was then that he discovered he had forgotten his repair kit, so he pushed his bicycle on to the sub-office. There, his friends teased him: 'How come? Sumiteru the speed merchant trudging round on foot.' He laughed with them; he would always, he knew, be able to outpace them all. Sumiteru propped his bike against the wall and walked off to deliver a few more letters. He noticed that the sky had clouded over. Fine too early, he thought to himself.

Back at the post office he borrowed a repair kit and set about mending the puncture. As he worked, the air-raid siren began to wail. Bock's Car was approaching from the north at a height of ten thousand metres. Sumiteru took little notice; he was used to the siren by now. He had just finished the repair job when, shortly before eleven o'clock, the all-clear went. Inexplicably – for at that moment the B.29, its bombardier's eye glued to the cross-hairs of his Nordern bomb-sight, was beginning its run-up on Nagasaki.

Sumiteru still had a lot of mail in his bag; it was time he left.

'Ja itte kurukara!' 'Goodbye fellows,' he called to his friends. 'I'll be back shortly.' He noticed that one of them, glass in hand, had slipped out through the back door to the water fountain to get a drink. It was to be his last. Sumiteru jumped on his bike and pedalled off to rejoin Route 206, lined there with pine trees; around the trunk of each, to keep the earth moist, lay a heap of boulders. He rode past a score of houses – no mail for them – then came to three more, standing in a row. Stopping at the middle one, he pushed the door open and dropped a couple of letters on the floor. 'Postman!' he called and heard a voice answer from somewhere inside, '*Arigato*,' thank you. A few yards further on, on the right, a narrow street led towards the *Sumiyoshi-jinja*, the local temple, and, further on, the Mitsubishi women workers' dormitory, where he had letters to deliver. As he turned into the street, he saw children in white shirts playing; they saw him too – he was their friend who passed by every day. They waved to him: 'Hullo Sumiteru, see you tomorrow.'

At that instant, the children and everything else around him disappeared in a blinding flash, bluish-white, like a gigantic arc-lamp, and accompanied by deafening, unearthly thunder – survivors would remember it as *pika-don*, the flash-boom. Then all was dust and darkness as a wind more violent than any typhoon blasted Sumiteru off his bicycle and hurled him to the ground some metres away. Through the murk, he glimpsed small white shapes, reminding him of leaves scattered by an autumn wind, being swept along the ground until they came to rest and lay still.

Before he hit the ground, something like a cannon-ball struck Sumiteru in the back – it was one of the boulders from the heap around the pine tree on the corner. For some moments, he lay still, wondering whether he was alive or dead. Then he became aware of an odd sensation – the earth was trembling beneath him. He realized he must still be alive. Immediately he was seized by the fear that he might after all die, there, in the road. He forced himself to think. 'No,' he murmured aloud, 'No, I'm not going to die, not here. I refuse.'

As he lay, trying to collect his thoughts, he dimly heard the sound of an aeroplane high overhead. It was Bock's Car, very low on fuel, on its way back to a forced landing at Okinawa. The crew were congratulating each other on a job well done. Someone called the bombardier on the intercom. 'Hey, Bea, you just killed a hundred thousand Japs.' Among them were those white objects looking like leaves scattered before the wind. They were the children who had just waved to Sumiteru.

It must have been more than a minute before Sumiteru felt the earth tremors die away. He forced himself to stand up and it was only then that he saw how terrible were his injuries. He could not know that he had received a heavy dose of radiation – gamma-rays and neutrons – but what was visible was awful enough. The skin of his left arm had been scorched off and hung down in shreds from his finger tips. The left side of his chest looked as if it had been clawed by some monstrous beast. He passed the back of his right hand across his back and saw it was a sticky mess of blood and dust. The skin had been flayed clean off his back, from his neck to his waistline, where it hung down, parchment-coloured, like a ragged length of cloth. The hideous appearance of his small body left Sumiteru unmoved. Nor did he feel any sensation of pain, not even from the heavy blow he had received from the flying boulder. Mentally, physically, he had been shocked beyond all feeling.

Sumiteru looked dazedly about him. Not far away lay the wreck of his red bike; it reminded him of twisted candy. His post-bag was empty and the remaining letters, done up in packets, were strewn among the débris lying in the street. Methodically, he gathered them up and put them back in the bag, saying to himself: 'I must get them delivered somehow.' His cap had been blown off and was nowhere to be found. Sumiteru's one object now was to reach the Mitsubishi tor-pedo factory a couple of hundred metres up the road and there get help. He knew he was in a bad state, but how bad he could not be sure. He must somehow get to the factory, otherwise he might die there among the rubble, among all the others already dead and dying.

63

The flames from nearby buildings permeated the darkness with a wan, yellowish light. Summarily, he took stock of the desolation around him. The houses he had passed just before the explosion were shattered and on fire, but by some freak, the devastating shock-wave had left almost intact the house where he had just dropped two letters. He hoped the owner of the voice inside was alive, but could not raise the strength to find out. The houses on each side, however, were in ruins and the occupants probably dead. In the streets now strewn with rubble and barely recognizable, lay scores of dead and injured. Most of them were horribly burnt, some were charred black and stiffened into weird and supplicating attitudes. Everywhere people, injured by blast, by glass and fallen masonry, desiccated by the searing heat, were calling for help. Their piteous cries rang in Sumiteru's ears but he could not answer them. That caused him no pang of guilt or remorse; the only person he was capable of helping was himself.

On the hill, Sumiteru had learnt what it meant to draw on his last ounce of strength. Now, grievously wounded and lost in a wilderness of shattered, burning houses he would have to do the same. He must push himself, force one foot in front of the other, to get himself to the torpedo works before he collapsed. He felt as if he were walking in his sleep until, in front of the Mitsubishi women's dormitory, he heard cries, louder than ever, around him. Women, their clothing burnt off, their hair singed off the scalp, staggered blindly round in circles, hysterically imploring help and, more urgently, water. 'Water, water, give us something to drink.' It seemed to Sumiteru that he was in a terrifying nightmare. His feet would not advance, he felt impotent, rooted to the spot, struggling vainly to drag his mind and his body away from that infernal scene. At last, he forced his eyes from those poor, demented women and fixed them again on the street, barely discernible beneath the rubble, which would lead him to the torpedo factory. It was less than a hundred metres away. He moved forward again, stumbling through wreckage, choked by dust and oblivious of the dead and the injured until at last he dragged his small body up to the entrance of one of the tunnels of the factory. There, he collapsed on to a bench.

Since the lighting had failed, it was darker within than without. Through the gloom, he could make out a few people, apparently uninjured and, to his mind, surprisingly calm. Working in the tunnels, they had been isolated from the horror further down the valley. A woman worker came to Sumiteru, bowed and said kindly, 'You poor boy . . . '

Sumiteru, bowing in turn, begged her anxiously: 'Water, please, something to drink.'

The woman brought him water in a small cup, apologizing: 'There is no more; the mains have been cut.' She held the cup to his lips and helped him to drink.

Sumiteru felt he was at last in safe hands. He asked her politely, with another bow: 'Please, will you cut off the skin hanging from my back and arms?' The woman went and groped in a cupboard, returning with a pair of scissors. She wiped them clean on a corner of Sumiteru's shirt, the remains of which were hanging round his neck. As best she could, she tidied up Sumiteru's lacerated body. Then she cut off his shirt, dipping it into a can of motor-oil, smeared the lubricant all over his raw flesh, dust, blood and all. Sumiteru felt no pain, but the whole revolting business was too much for him. He passed out.

When, a few minutes later, he came round again, a workman was bending over him, a kind-faced man who said: 'Come on, son, we're going to get you out of here. The place is full of explosives and it's not the place for you.' He went on, 'I'll carry you up on the hillside,' and with the woman helping, hoisted Sumiteru on to his back. The hill above the tunnels was grassy with many trees. The climb was steep but short. Ten minutes later, the workman, having found a small patch of level ground, laid Sumiteru gently on his stomach, in the grass. It was still dark, with the sky obscured by smoke and dust, through which only the sun, a dark red, unshining orb, was visible. But a breeze was blowing from the southwest; it kept the flies away from Sumiteru's raw flesh and did something else, too, which probably saved his life. Black rain, the same greasy, radioactive drops which had fallen on Hiroshima, began to fall from the sky over Nagasaki. Sumiteru, dazed as he was, had never noticed the mushroom-shaped atomic cloud, kilometres high in the air above the city. The wind carried it away eastwards and its deadly black rain pelted down on the people of Nishiyama, a pretty suburb in an adjoining valley.

It was some time after midday. Sumiteru, flat on his stomach in the grass, was capable of only one thought: I must not die. Further than that, his mind would not function – until, round about three o'clock, he realized that he was not alone. Painfully he raised his head and looked around. He saw men and women labouring up the steep hill towards him; there must have been some thirty in all. Sumiteru could see from their burnt and mutilated bodies that they were in agony, perhaps their last. He wanted to help but could only remain inert, watching them until they came and dropped down in the grass around him, groaning and crying out for water. As the afternoon wore on, their plaintive cries grew less and Sumiteru knew that some of them must already be dead. He wondered how much longer it would be before he, too, died. He craved for water and something to eat; it had been hours since he had enjoyed those two lunch-boxes of Oba-chan.

Towards evening, he could hear a train come puffing down the line a few hundred metres away, from the northern suburb of Michinoo, venturing cautiously down the valley as far as the track held, which was just a little further down from the torpedo factory. Word came to the people on the hillside above the factory that they should make their way down to the train which would evacuate them. Sumiteru could not move. A few others got up unsteadily and tried to walk. Not one of them made it beyond a few paces; they fell to the ground again and lay still.

Past the folds in the hills, Sumiteru, craning his neck, could see down the valley. The murk had lifted somewhat, revealing a sea of flame. The hills, his beloved hills, were on fire and below them, Nagasaki was itself a brazier.

66

9

The bomb, missing as it did by three kilometres the intended aiming point down-town, had devastated the target, 'Nagasaki urban area' even more thoroughly than Truman and his planners had hoped. It had transformed the whole length of the Urakami valley into a valley of death. That pleasant valley, generously endowed by nature with flowers and forests and wild-life, a valley animated by human life and industry, had, in a sudden, blinding flash, become a sombre, featureless desert of dust and burning ruins, strewn with charred and mutilated corpses. The living, those who could stand or even crawl, fled from the inferno down towards the cool waters of the river; soon afterwards the Urakami was crammed with dead, floating down towards the harbour and the open sea, departed spirits but who, with no Obon festival for the dead that August, would miss the usual joyous send-off to their faraway home across the waters. At present, they formed a mass of anonymous souls despatched, without further ceremony, into oblivion.

There was strange irony in Bock's Car's faulty aiming. Down-town Nagasaki, though spared the worst of the blast, did not escape the atomb bomb's thermal radiation; so intense were its heat waves that, even at three kilometres from burstpoint, they penetrated buildings and set palm trees and telegraph poles smouldering. Two hours later, flames began licking round them. The southwesterly wind kindled them into a blaze and sent wild-fire sweeping through the downtown area and back up to the top of the valley, gutting the ruins of buildings already demolished by blast, reducing them to ashes. In that roadless wilderness where water-mains were cut, the few surviving fire-engines and their brass-helmeted crews were helpless.

Fate played many an unkind game in Nagasaki that day. The son of Thomas Glover, Tomisaburo – whose father had done so much to make Nagasaki prosper – was still living there. That morning of the atom bomb, his wife Waka had gone shopping. She never returned; her husband, after searching vainly for her, shot himself.

Husbands and wives, parents and children, brothers and sisters who, at the beginning of that day, had bid one another *sayonara*, goodbye, as they left for work or school, were never to meet again; thousands of families were torn apart by the sudden death that smote Nagasaki in the middle of the morning. Masato Araki, a young official working at the town hall, had the impression that a hundred flash-bulbs had gone off in his face, that a typhoon had hit the city. Though badly shaken, he was far more concerned for his father who had just been transferred to a new job at the Mitsubishi electric foundry. While the fire which raged through the down-town area drove Masato to take refuge in the hills, his thoughts all that night were for the parent he had left behind. His father, unknown to him, lay with scores of others, charred beyond recognition, among the ruins of the foundry.

Mitsubishi had been swept clean out of the valley, save for its torpedo factory, tunnelled into the hill on which Sumiteru now lay. Of the Mitsubishi steel works, downstream from the electric foundry, there remained only a huge skeleton of twisted girders with, strangely enough, its dozen tall chimneys still standing gaunt and more or less erect.

Nineteen-year-old Yukie Tsuji worked at the factory as a secretary. She had arrived that morning, as usual, at a quarter past seven. The air-raid alarm had sent everyone running for the underground shelter but when, just before eleven o'clock, the all-clear sounded, Yukie hurried back to the office; she had yet to prepare the workers' lunch tickets. She then heard the sound of an aircraft. She went to the office door and stared up into the sky. Suddenly she was blinded by a vivid, bluish-white flash. Her bare arms and face felt as if starch had suddenly dried on them. Yukie fainted, then woke up to find that she was lying beneath the ruins of the office building. Other workers came to her rescue and pulled her out. Her face and arms were hurting badly. Though almost blinded, she could dimly see that the skin was hanging from her finger-tips. She was laid on a door which had been extricated from the ruins. On it, workmen carried her four kilometres through the ruins of the city, back to her home, in Nameshi-Urakami.

It was there, at the district post office that morning, that Sumiteru had waved goodbye to his comrades – for the last time. Most of them were now dead.

Below the steel works, in Saiwai-machi, another Mitsubishi plant had been blasted into ruins. In the nearby prisoner-of-war camp, 'Fukuoka No 14', several men, including Americans, British and Dutch, were killed outright. The atom bomb, with its 'devastating strength', was no more a respecter of friends and allies, than it was of non-combatants.

A strange chance had saved Sid Lawrence from being among the dead. For some days he had watched every morning as an American reconnaissance plane had over-flown Nagasaki at a great height, gleaming like silver in the blue and trailing a long wake of white vapour. Not once did he notice any opposition from Japanese anti-aircraft or fighters.

On the morning of 9 August he was one of a working party of half-a-dozen men detailed to unload rubble from lorries and stack it in one big heap. They were guarded by a single Japanese soldier. Hearing aircraft, Sid looked up. The sky was now partly covered with high cloud, but he could pick out not the usual solitary plane, but three planes. Over the city the two to the right and left broke away, while the centre one continued on a steady course. Suddenly it glinted a bright silver and Sid thought: That could be the bomb doors opening. For some seconds he followed the plane as it turned away in a dive. During those moments Sid, under the eye of the sentry, was throwing his basket of rubble on to the heap while on the far side of it the other men were loading theirs from a lorry. A blinding flash filled the sky and following it, a rushing wind and the long rumbling of thunder. Not far away a huge cloud of orange-black smoke swelled from the ground, rising and spreading. From it there spouted more smoke, a swirling column spiralling skywards. The sky darkened and Sid thought: It looks as if the sun's going to be blotted out for ever. He heard the Japanese soldier screaming, '*Nanio*! What the hell is it?' Sid shouted back '*Arimus-sen Haiti-san*: I don't know, Mr Soldier'; whereupon the terrified man threw down his rifle and took to his heels.

In a daze, Sid staggered round to the other side of the heap of rubble. There were his five companions, on their knees, motionless, without a scratch on them. They were all dead. He had been saved by the mound of rubble. He picked up the sentry's rifle, made his way back to the camp and handed it in to the sentry. Not that they mattered much now – there was nothing left of the camp for them to guard.

North of the hypocentre, where the River Otonashigawa flows into the Urakami, the Mitsubishi Ordnance factory was in ruins. Opposite it stood the Junshin High School for girls, a Catholic convent, from which third-year students had been conscripted to work in the Ordnance factory. Proud of serving their country, they sang as usual on their way to work that morning:

> We, the young budding cherries
> With the blood of youth stirring
> In our hearts
> This is our sacred duty
> To give ourselves joyfully
> In this time of crisis.

Truman's atom bomb consummated their sacrifice. Two hundred of them perished in the ruins of the Ordnance factory. Three more were found dead at the roadside, near the Isabaya bridge, laid out in spring kimonos by some unknown sympathizer. Those three had been on their way that morning to help in the School for the Blind.

By some miracle another conscript student employed at the Ordnance factory, fifteen-year-old Senzi Yamaguti, escaped death; no doubt because he had been put to work with a small gang outside, digging a shelter trench. Spared as he was from the falling masonry which killed so many others, Senzi did not escape the direct effects of the bomb. Within a fraction of a second the *pika*, the flash, stabbed him like a white-hot poker in the eyes, as the blast knocked him out.

It must have been twenty minutes or so before he came to and noticed that everyone was making for the river, some two hundred metres away. He followed, but the bridge was so crammed with people that Senzi, like hundreds of others, jumped into the water and somehow swam among the drifting bodies to the other side. There he started climbing up the hill, till he came to a place where about three hundred others had sat down to rest or simply collapsed unconscious. Senzi stayed with them. His right arm and that side of his neck and face were burnt raw; his right ear had been almost burnt away.

By the evening Senzi reckoned that at least half of those people on the hillside had died. With an effort he got up and walked down the hillside to the railway track, near the Showenzi temple, beyond which the line on to Nagasaki had been torn up.

Soon, a train came. Willing hands helped young Senzi aboard, though no one could do anything for his massive third-degree burns. The train moved off northwards, up the valley and beyond it, stopping at Michinoo and every other station *en route* to pick up or discharge the wounded. One and a half hours later it steamed into Omura, sixty kilometres away. Senzi climbed down and, still half blind and dazed, collapsed on the platform. It would have been bad enough if the tender, but unbroken, skin of his left cheek had struck the ground, but he did not fall that way; it was the raw flesh of his right cheek and the pathetic stump of his ear which hit the dust-covered concrete. From that moment Senzi's agony began. An ambulance rushed him to the naval hospital where his wounds were daubed with a green liquid, and he received an anti-tetanus injection. Then he fell into a semi-coma in which he was to remain for six weeks.

Most grievous was the destruction done to Nagasaki's schools, its places of worship, its hospitals. The primary schools of Yamazato, Shiroyama, Fuchi, and the secondary schools of Keiho and Chinzei, both the technical and the commercial schools were all destroyed and gutted by fire. Teachers and their pupils, children and teenagers, thousands of them, died together in the ruins of their classrooms. The medical college and its hospital collapsed under the blast and caught fire. Doctors, students and patients trapped beneath the ruins were burnt to death.

An ex-student of the medical college, twenty-nine-year-old Tatsuichiro Akizuki, as diminutive as he was dynamic and full of fun, was resident doctor at Urakami First hospital, installed in a Franciscan monastery on nearby Motohara hill and familiarly known as St Francis hospital. That morning of the ninth, the doctor went about his work as usual, humming cheerfully. He heard the air-raid alarm, then, before eleven, the all-clear. As planes seemed to be still overhead, he quickly withdrew the needle from a patient upon whom he had begun a pneumo-thorax operation. At that instant an intense blue-white light blotted everything from his view and he was thrown to the floor. Then, suddenly, it was dark and clouds of dust were pouring in through the shattered windows. For twenty minutes, Doctor Akizuki and the nursing staff, dazed as they were by the blast, worked frantically to evacuate patients from the burning hospital. Then the smoke and dust cleared somewhat and the doctor could see not far away the Convent of the Holy Cross and Urakami cathedral in ruins; both buildings were blazing furiously. Trapped within the cathedral, twenty priests and two hundred worshippers had perished instantly, as they knelt at confession – in less than a week, it would be the Feast of the Assumption.

Following the explosion, crowds of bemused and injured people had struggled up from the valley to the St Francis hospital where they begged for water and succour for their burns and wounds. Hundreds more made for the precincts of the blazing cathedral, there to pray for deliverance or breathe their last.

A few hundred metres to the east of Urakami cathedral, on the lower slopes of Mount Konpira, nine-year-old Tadashi and his sister Toshiko, were playing. Tadashi had climbed to the top of a tall pine tree, and was clinging on, his arms round the trunk, when he heard Toshiko shout: 'Planes, quick, Tadashi, come down.' Before he had time to move, Tadashi felt as if his eyes had been suddenly burnt out. Somehow he managed to slither down the tree; he rolled down the slope and came to a stop, not knowing whether he was dead or alive, until he heard his sister's voice again: 'Come on, Tadashi.' They both raced down the hill to their home in Takao-machi. They found the house only partly damaged, sheltered as it was by a high bank, but every other building in sight was a heap of ruins.

When they had left home that morning to play on the hill, their mother, clad in head-cloth, blouse and *mompei*, baggy trousers, was just leaving to gather potatoes in the fields. Their father, Kokurawa, had begun work putting up a new potting shed. Soon after starting, he had taken off his shirt, so warm was it that day. Tadashi called out *sayonara* to them both. His parents were always good to him and he loved them because they worked so hard. Two hours or so had gone by since then and now Tadashi was standing over his father, who lay half conscious in the débris of his potting shed, the bare skin of his chest and stomach branded a purplish-brown. Some moments later, his mother came in from the fields. She walked unsteadily and Tadashi could see that her clothes were badly scorched, her bare arms and hands burnt raw; the flayed skin hung like a frill from each of her finger-tips. Having no medicines, Tadashi, helped by Toshiko, dabbed persimmon juice and aloes on their parents' wounds and covered them with leaves. Then, despite his pain, Tadashi's father went to join the others, helping to pull the injured from the wreckage of neighbouring houses.

Tadashi was soon to discover how cruelly the atom bomb

had afflicted his own family. His married sister Saku, who lived not far from the Urakami cathedral, was shopping that morning in the quiet streets of Takao-machi when suddenly it seemed to her that the sun had fallen out of the sky with a deafening thunder-clap. Saku was struck with terror; mercifully, though, she was unhurt. She began running as fast as her trembling legs would carry her back to her home where she had left her three little girls at play. The *pika-don* had put an end to their games. Saku found two small, charred and lifeless bodies in the ruins of her house. They were the youngest of the three. It was hours before she found her eldest child, a girl of ten; she was barely alive.

As he finished his rescue work, word came to Kokurawa about his daughter Saku, and he insisted on setting off to get news of her. Tadashi accompanied him. They had not far to walk, but the going was painfully hard, the streets blocked by heaps of dead and the ground so hot that Tadashi, barefoot, had to jump from corpse to corpse as if they were stepping-stones. Of Saku they found no trace, other than the ruins of her home. She and her husband, Ideka, had already carried away the bodies of their two little girls and were still out searching for the third.

Kokurawa's cup of sorrow, shared by his family, was not yet full. Next day a neighbour of his married son, Hidesaku, called and, bowing gravely, announced that Hidesaku's wife and three children had all been found dead. Hidesaku, away at the war, would remain unaware of the catastrophe until, weeks later, he returned to find that he was the sole living member of his young family. It was the same with his sister Saku and her husband; the same, too, with countless thousands of others who were at the front or who had simply bid *sayonara* to their families that morning, as they left home to go to work. The atom bomb's 'devastating strength' had bereft them of their entire family.

Manifestly, the fanaticism of the Tokyo war-lords, countered by Truman's precipitate use of the atom bomb (which he, the ex-gunnery officer, stupidly called 'just another piece of artillery') had between them accomplished a shameful massacre, a massacre of whole families, of school-children and their teachers, of the sick and the faithful and those who administered to them, of ordinary people whose business was the care and love of their children, the family shopping, the patient tending of the garden plot, the potting shed. Little people. And besides them were the wild-life, the flowers and the forests, and the history which composed the alluring beauty of Nagasaki. A single aircraft, a single bomb, had obliterated all that. Among the tens of thousands of people it had killed, 150 only wore the uniform of the imperial armed forces.

Deaths among factory workers (if they must count as combatants) amounted to 13 per cent of the total; they included, of course, the two hundred girls from the Junshin High School and hundreds more conscripted students, killed and wounded, like fifteen-year-old Senzi Yamaguti.

The atom bomb had proved itself the most efficient method of mass slaughter and devastation so far devised. But the means of delivering it by aircraft were still rudimentary, as was the bomb itself. The Nagasaki plutonium bomb, though nearly twice as powerful as the uranium one of Hiroshima, was but a mini-bomb, capable of destroying only one city – and its inhabitants – at a time. There was plenty of room for improvement, as time would show, until the practical limit of destruction might one day be reached – the planet Earth itself.

IO

Night fell upon Nagasaki and the sky reflected the gory red of the conflagration below. The city, from the port right up the length of the valley almost to the hill where Sumiteru lay, was engulfed in fire. About midnight, he heard a plane approaching – enemy no doubt. It circled low, then began machine-gunning people who, searching for their relatives, were clearly silhouetted against the flames. A stray bullet, ricocheting off a rock near where Sumiteru lay, made him cry out in anguish: 'Why must you go on shooting at us now we are dead?' He felt intensely lonely; his thoughts turned to Oba-chan and he prayed that she had reached home without trouble after leaving him that morning at the main post office. But were she and Ji-san safely beyond reach of the flames?

In Tokyo that morning, at precisely eleven o'clock, Prime Minister Suzuki opened the emergency meeting he had called of the Big Six, all of whom had already heard about Russia's declaration of war. Suzuki came quickly to the point: 'I have concluded that our only alternative is to accept the Potsdam Proclamation and terminate the war.' The military members, War Minister General Anami, the most bellicose of the three, and the Army and Navy Chiefs of Staff, General Umezu and Admiral Toyoda, remonstrated fiercely. They insisted that the war be continued on Japanese soil. As they were arguing, a message was brought in and handed to Suzuki; it announced that Nagasaki had just been hit by an atom bomb. The news was shattering, coming as it did on top of Hiroshima. But for the military it did not mean the end. Their battle-cry had not changed: 'A hundred million will die together!' On the other hand, Russia's declaration of war earlier that morning was a

decisive blow. It meant the end of all their hopes of a negotiated peace, of an honourable *samurai*-style surrender. It meant
the end of the war. There only remained one alternative as
Suzuki had just told them, disgraceful though it might appear
to the military – unconditional surrender.

Heated discussion among the Big Six continued until, at two
o'clock in the afternoon, Suzuki, in despair, adjourned the
meeting. It was obvious to him that there now remained but
one solution: the Emperor himself must make the decision. It
would mean breaking with tradition, but the Emperor, after
Suzuki had told him of the impasse, was willing to defy the old
order.

During a meeting of the full Cabinet that afternoon, Suzuki
made yet another attempt to secure a decision through the
constitutional process, but the military persisted in their refusal to yield to the civilian ministers. The latter were for
unconditional surrender, arguing that, apart from the fact that
Japan now possessed no fleet, no effective air defences and
precious little in the way of oil and munitions, the people were
on the verge of starvation and had no stomach for the final
show-down on Japanese soil, so essential to the military in
order to save face – their own face.

Anami dismissed their arguments; he was even mad enough
to claim that, despite the Russians, despite the two atomic
bombs and a firm promise of more, it was still possible to
reverse the situation and pull victory out of defeat. 'We must
fight to the end, no matter what the odds.' The real truth was
that Japan had nothing to fight with. By 11 p.m., still without
any decision on surrender, the meeting broke up.

Suzuki immediately arranged for yet another imperial conference. It was now for the Emperor himself to decide. It was
just before midnight when his Imperial Majesty, looking tired
and anxious, faced the Big Six in the sombre, stuffy conference
room of the *obunko*, the royal underground shelter. Each
minister in turn stated his opinion. Foreign Minister Togo was
for surrender; Navy Minister Yonai agreed. Umezu declared
sottishly that Japan would counter-attack, that further atomic

raids would be contained – a vain pretension considering that American bombers had for weeks been buzzing the capital, Tokyo, without opposition and in the last few days had attacked with impunity Hiroshima and Nagasaki. The third of the military triumvirate, Admiral Toyoda, ignoring America's stated intention of utterly destroying Japanese cities, was idiotic enough to say: 'We do not believe we will be completely defeated.'

The fanatical Anami would have nothing to do with surrender unless the Army were allowed to remain under his control. 'If not,' he said, 'Japan must continue fighting and find life in death.' His voice rose as he talked of 'our hundred million people'; they were ready to die, he ranted, for the honour and glory of Japan.

It was now two o'clock in the morning of 10 August – high time, after nearly three hours of futile argument, for Suzuki to pray the Emperor to express his wishes. Suzuki bowed low and the Emperor rose to his feet. His voice was strained. 'Continuing the war,' he said, 'would mean the destruction of the nation. I cannot bear to see my innocent people suffer any longer.' Ending the war was the only way of relieving the nation from its terrible distress. Nearly overcome with emotion, he managed to stammer: 'I swallow my tears and give my sanction to the proposal to accept the allied proclamation.' His words signified more than mere approval. They were an imperial command: Japan will surrender. The war-lords, Anami, Umezu and Toyoda, stricken almost to the point of collapse, bowed low in obeisance. It was 2.30 a.m. on the morning of the 10th.

At that moment, on the hill above the torpedo factory at Nagasaki, rain was beginning to fall. Sumiteru reacted instinctively. He wriggled a few metres towards a bush and tore off one of its big leaves. Holding it cup-shaped, he managed to catch a few drops and get them past his lips. He repeated the movement three or four times until his strength failed. Those few meagre drops refreshed him slightly; he got some relief, too, by moving his head first to one side, then the other, so that the rain could splash on each of his cheeks. But on the raw flesh of his back and arms, smeared with engine-oil, the rain left no sensation.

During those long hours while General Anami in Tokyo had been demanding a last sacrifice from the nation, Sumiteru had lain in the grass, caring nothing in his agony for the honour and glory of Japan. The moaning of the injured around him had grown fainter; most of those poor people, he was sure, were now beyond all earthly cares.

Sumiteru fell asleep and slept on until, a couple of hours later, day broke and the red glow faded from the sky leaving an overcast of smoke and dust still hanging over Nagasaki. On the hillside all was now silent. Raising himself as best he could on his hands and the unburnt surface of his arms, Sumiteru looked around him. Not a sign of life showed in any of the others and he realized that all of them were indeed dead. Yet the horror of lying there, surrounded by thirty corpses, never occurred to him. He could think only of one thing; he must not die as they had. Now in full possession of his senses, he noticed a persimmon tree some ten metres from where he lay. Its fruit, he knew, was far from ripe, but it might help a little to assuage his raging thirst. Clutching the grass with his hands, he pulled himself forward, pushing at the same time with his legs and feet. Gradually he slithered towards the tree. Then, propping himself up on his left hand, he reached up with his right, grabbed at a branch and pulled it down towards him. He managed to pull off three berries before letting go. With a good deal of fumbling, he pushed one of the berries into his mouth, bit fiercely into it and sucked.

The sensation of biting the hard, unripe fruit and swallowing the bitter juice, though it made him wince, brought him some hard-won satisfaction. He spat out the remains and repeated the process with the second berry, then the third.

Sumiteru felt a little better. From where he lay, unable to move off his stomach, he could look down the hill and watch the relief train not far below coming and going, evacuating survivors northwards out of the valley. He could see, too, scores of survivors lying around the entrance to the tunnels of the torpedo factory. Watching avidly as they were fed rice balls and soup, Sumiteru tried to call out and attract the attention of the rescue teams. His voice was too weak to carry that far. Frustrated and miserable, he turned his face away. He had been forgotten, taken no doubt for one of those thirty dead in whose midst he lay.

Once again the idea came stronger than ever, into Sumiteru's mind: I refuse to die. Fleeting thoughts occurred to him, of the soldiers who had resisted so desperately in the Pacific Islands. His courage returned; he had lived all his young life on the hill and knew how much it demanded of all the creatures, human and animal, who lived – and survived – there. The hill had hardened him; he would survive – he was sure of it. He shut out of his mind those more fortunate victims below who were being fed and succoured. He would somehow survive on his own.

Again he raised himself and looked around him. Some way away, it must be at least a hundred metres, he could make out a small farmhouse between the trees and clumps of bamboo. Gathering his post-bag to him, he began to wriggle forward. It would take time to reach it, but the slope helped. After advancing some metres, a bamboo thicket barred his way and it seemed that he was defeated. He tried to hoist himself upright, but collapsed, feeling an excruciating pain in his thigh as a broken bamboo stem pierced his burnt flesh. After lying still for some time waiting for the pain to subside, he started again to wriggle forward on his belly, gradually working his way round the thicket. Dragging himself on his arms, pushing with his legs and feet, he at last reached the door of the farmhouse. It was open, but inside there was no sign of life. A large earthenware vessel stood by the door and next to it a bamboo bowl. Sumiteru's fingers closed on it and he forced himself upright; the big vessel was nearly full of water, some of which he baled out and drank, splashing more over his face and body. It would have to do too, for food, for there was nothing to eat in sight.

The farmhouse had been badly damaged by the blast. Sumiteru decided it was unsafe to shelter there and wriggled outside again, making towards a tree, another persimmon. Once beneath its shade, he collapsed from his exertions and lay still, waiting for his strength to return. Then, with some difficulty, he struggled out of his breeches and puttees, rolling them into a bundle. Only now did he notice that the seat of his khaki breeches was burnt; his white underpants, still intact, had protected him from further burns. Sumiteru laid his head on his makeshift pillow and soon he was asleep. He would probably have slept on right through the afternoon and night into the following dawn, had he not been awakened just before dark. A man was standing over him – a Korean workman from the torpedo factory. Without a word he pulled Sumiteru's breeches and leggings from under his head and made off. Sumiteru had not the strength to resist. He fell asleep once more and slept on.

Far away in Tokyo General Anami and the Army were plotting to prolong the war, while in Washington Truman had ordered no quarter for the Japanese until they surrendered.

Sumiteru woke up with a start. It was early in the morning of the eleventh and a man of the rescue corps was prodding him with his boot, uncertain whether any life remained in that small and cruelly mutilated body. Sumiteru groaned; a few minutes later the rescue man, helped by another, picked up the boy and, without a word, laid him on the wooden door which they had removed from the entrance to the farmhouse.

Sumiteru asked them: 'Please take me to the Iwaya-machi post office.' There, he still had to deliver more letters; they were in his post-bag, from which he refused to be separated. He was hoping, too, to send a message to Oba-chan, but on arriving at the post office he found only chaos; all the lines were cut. He handed over his mail and the rescue men carried him on the few hundred metres more to Michinoo station.

The message that Sumiteru wanted to send to Oba-chan had already reached her. His friend Honda, who had left the main post office with him that fateful morning, had ridden on much further up-town. Unhurt by the explosion, he made his way back down Route 206, searching for Sumiteru; he came upon his mangled red post office bicycle, not far away he found his cap. Honda pushed his own bicycle on through the rubble and flames and up the hill to Oba-chan's home, which, apart from its few missing tiles and shattered windows, was still intact. Had the B.29's aim been accurate, Oba-chan would probably have been killed, Sumiteru certainly spared.

Honda showed Sumiteru's cap to Oba-chan and, as he drank green tea with her and Ji-san, explained how he had found it, without a sign of Sumiteru. When he had finished, the old couple bowed gratefully to him, concealing their fear. As soon as the boy was gone, Ji-san set off to look for Sumiteru.

Laboriously, he picked his way for five kilometres or so among the clutter of blazing ruins, his feet hurting from the scorching hot ground despite his sandals, until he came to the shattered remains of the Sumiyoshi-cho sub-post office. There was no one there. So, with the hundreds of others who like him were engaged in the sorrowful quest for their missing relatives, Ji-san searched the district vainly until nightfall, when fires lit up the city. Even then he did not stop until, exhausted, he went and lay down in the ricefields beside the Urakami, where he slept. Around him in the darkness there flickered hundreds of small fires. The dead were being cremated where they lay.

He rose again early next morning, and all through that day wandered among the ruins of Sumiyoshi-cho, calling Sumiteru by name, scrutinizing each one of the dead and injured, pursuing his fruitless search. Believing that Sumiteru must be lying somewhere around the sub-post office, it never occurred to Ji-san to push on further up the valley as far as the torpedo works. He slept that night once more beside the Urakami.

Further downstream, amidst the ruins of Fukuoka No 14 prisoner-of-war camp, Sid Lawrence found it impossible to sleep. Early that day he and two other prisoners, guarded by a couple of soldiers, had been detailed as a search party with orders to rescue any survivors they might find in the worst damaged districts. Sid had done similar jobs in the blitzes on London and Sheffield; during the bombing of Singapore he had seen the streets littered with dead and dismembered bodies; in Java, too, he had helped with the dead and the dying. But Nagasaki, in its sheer, inexplicable horror, surpassed anything that he had so far witnessed. What unearthly device could have wrought such destruction? Sid had not yet heard of Hiroshima.

A few survivors were still wandering about; to Sid they looked like zombies; walking dead. The search party came across some children. In the past, Sid had found himself helping screaming children into lorries to be evacuated, but these children were not screaming; they were silent except for

83

an occasional whimper. He came upon a little girl sitting on the ground, half facing him. '*Koy, koy,* come here, come,' he invited her, but she did not move. He went to pick her up. Later, he recalled, 'As I stood over her I came over sick with horror.' From where he had been standing she had appeared to be unhurt, but now he could see that the other side of her small body was charred black. Where her right eye had been there now remained only a blank, white cavity.

Sid carried her over to one of the soldiers. As he walked he noticed that at the side of the concrete road there were dark shadows. People must have been walking there, but of their bodies there was no trace; they had been burnt to ashes. He carried a stick to help him as he clambered over the débris towards a large, gutted building, now a tangle of twisted iron girders. He struck a fallen girder with his stick and, to his amazement, cut clean through it; the bomb's thermal rays had reduced it to dust. Again he wondered: What in God's name could have done that?

He looked about him. Some trees had been snapped in two, others were still standing, but with one side scorched as if they had been whitewashed, the other with foliage and bark apparently unharmed. It was the same on the foot-hills running up from the valley; one slope was dead white, or charred, or still smouldering, the other green with vegetation. The smell which pervaded the air of Nagasaki reminded him of something between grilled sardines and the strange odour given off by an overheating dentist's drill. It was nauseating.

Sid grasped the hand of one of the soldiers, an ex-school teacher, and exclaimed, 'What have we done to you?'

'What have we done to each other?' replied the soldier, and burst into tears.

That night Sid lay awake, unable to take his mind off the events of the last few days. Some way upstream, beside the Urakami river, Ji-san, despite his anxiety for Sumiteru, slept soundly.

When dawn came on the eleventh he felt more determined than ever to succeed in his efforts to trace Sumiteru; if the boy

84

could not be found in the Sumiyoshi-cho, he would go and enquire at the other sub-office in Iwaya-machi, a kilometre or so down the valley, where he knew Sumiteru always called on his way back down-town. Ji-san's intuition was right. Of the Iwaya-machi office, less than a kilometre from the hypocentre, nothing remained, but the postmaster, who had survived, gave Ji-san information that raised his hopes. Sumiteru had been brought there, very badly injured, a few hours earlier, and after leaving his letters had been taken on by train to Michinoo, one stop further up the line.

Ji-san jumped on the next train and came to Michinoo. There, at the back of the little timber-built station, he found Sumiteru lying on his stomach in the shade of a tall tree amongst a pitiful heap of mutilated humanity. Ji-san, for all his oriental impassivity, could hardly restrain his feelings at the sight of his grandson. Three days ago, he had gone off to work, a lively, cheerful youth. Now he lay there, a small, inert heap of blistered, rotting flesh. The old man bent down and said into the boy's ear: 'It's Ji-san. You'll be all right, my son. I'll stay with you till you are well.' Sumiteru gave a little groan of recognition. He felt safe with Ji-san.

Soon afterwards Ji-san helped to carry him back into the next train. Filled with groaning wounded, heaped one against another on boards laid across the seats, it took them on to Isahaya, one of the evacuation centres, twenty kilometres north of Nagasaki. There, at the elementary school, Sumiteru was laid on a *tatami*, on the floor of one of the classrooms. Ji-san dossed down beside him. He was lucky to find the space, for all the schools of Isahaya were crammed with victims. As fast as they died and were carried away to be cremated, others took their place.

During the days that followed the annihilation of Nagasaki and the Emperor's command to surrender, the all-powerful leaders of the warring nations, at a safe distance in Washington and, slightly less so, in the underground bunkers in Tokyo, were apparently feeling no remorse at the massacres for which they were both responsible. In Tokyo, Anami and the Army were plotting a last, bloody battle on the Japanese mainland; in Washington, Truman had rejected the pleas of Stimson and Forrestal who begged him, with peace so close, to suspend, as a humane gesture, further air attacks against Japan. 'Out of the question,' replied Truman, first nuclear potentate, with power to destroy all who resisted him. The pressure on Japan, he ordained, must be kept up; 'conventional' bombing raids must continue relentlessly, more Japanese civilians be slain. Two more atomic bombs would be dropped, one on the thirteenth and the other on the sixteenth, if Japan did not surrender.

Japan, by the decision of its Prime Minister, had already surrendered before the atom bomb fell on Nagasaki; his decision was confirmed by the Emperor's command early on the tenth. It was now vital for the Tokyo government to get their message through to Washington without delay – otherwise a third atomic bomb might obliterate yet another Japanese city. To gain time, the surrender note was broadcast that morning by the Domei press agency. It was immediately picked up in Washington and in the early hours of the twelfth, Tokyo received the American reply. It accepted Japan's surrender and, in a rather roundabout way, the continuing status of the Emperor; this, said the American note, would be established by the freely expressed will of the Japanese people. The Emperor himself was satisfied; he trusted the wisdom and loyalty of his people, but when the full Cabinet met that afternoon, they could do nothing but argue and vacillate. Anami, needless to say, rejected any question of surrender. Further procrastination followed at a meeting next day of the Big Six, until Suzuki declared roundly: 'I have made up my mind to end the war.'

Meanwhile an army coup, to which Anami was privy even if he did not openly approve it, had been preparing. The military believed that the Emperor had been wrongly advised; he must be protected from his craven-hearted ministers, notably Suzuki, and persuaded to change his mind. Sensing that the army opposition was so strong, Suzuki convened another imperial conference. The Emperor would once again have to impose his authority on the unruly military. When the Emperor received the Cabinet at 10.50 a.m. on 14 August, Suzuki began by naming the principal opponents to surrender: Toyoda, Umezu and Anami. None of them would accept the American reply as a definite promise about the Emperor's future status. Given that uncertainty, all three demanded that the entire nation should be sacrificed in a last battle on the mainland.

The Emperor, in a voice full of emotion, then spoke. His own view, he said, had not changed. 'We cannot continue the war any longer.' He did not read in the American note any intention to eliminate *Kokutai*, the national essence, or to destroy the Japanese nation. With the horror of Hiroshima and Nagasaki so fresh in his mind, the Emperor went on: 'I cannot let my subjects suffer any longer. I wish to save the people at the risk of my own life. If the war continues, our entire nation will be laid waste; hundreds of thousands more will die.' He concluded with the command: 'It is my desire that all of you, my ministers of state, bow to my wishes and accept the allied reply forthwith.'

To allay people's surprise at his decision and to convince them that the government really had surrendered, he offered to make a broadcast to the nation. It was 11.30 a.m when, in the studios of the Japanese Broadcasting Corporation, the NHK, the Emperor began to record. He made two recordings; the problem then was to find a safe place to conceal the discs. Certainly the broadcasting station was not the right place, now that rumours of a military coup were rife. They were finally locked up in a safe in the Household Ministry inside the palace. Not many minutes later, the palace was cordoned off and occupied by rebel troops, who began a frantic search for the two discs. They could not be found and the troops were withdrawn.

The coup had failed. General Anami, on hearing the news, prepared himself for death. He drank *sake* with his brother-in-law Takeshita, one of the leaders of the coup, into the early hours of the next morning, the fifteenth. And he wrote a poem:

> Believing in the eternity of our Divine Land
> With my death I apologize to the Emperor
> For the great crime.

At about 4 a.m. Anami thrust a dagger into his abdomen, slashing to the right and straight up; it was *Kappuku*, the most agonizing way of committing *hara-kiri*.

Agonizing no less, Sumiteru, one of those hundred million whom Anami had wanted to sacrifice in a last futile bid to save his own and the Army's face, lay on the floor of the elementary school in Isahaya. His raw, burnt flesh, numb these last few days, had now become alive again and racked him with massive, excruciating pain.

At midday on 15 August the Emperor, whose royal symbol was the Crane, broadcast to the nation. He spoke in a thin, piping voice and expressed himself with the imperial 'We': 'We have decided to effect a settlement of the present situation by resorting to an extraordinary measure.' The enemy, he said, had used cruel bombs to kill and maim extremely large numbers of the innocent; if the war were continued, it would lead not only to the downfall of the nation, but also the destruction of all human civilization. He went on to announce that 'We' had given orders to 'Our' government to accept the allied terms of unconditional surrender. Millions of Japanese, standing with heads bowed or kneeling, listened incredulous to the voice of the Crane, tears streaming down their cheeks. Nowhere in the world had so many ever wept at once as at that moment in Japan.

In No 14 Fukuoka camp Sid and his comrades were gathered round a wireless set from which there came a high-pitched voice. Sid noticed an elderly Japanese woman standing in front of the set and continually bowing, as if she was a clockwork toy. The others asked him: 'What's going on? Who's speaking? What's he saying?' 'It's the Emperor of Japan and he's saying the war's over.' There was not a trace of excitement in Sid's voice. He spoke in a monotone, like a robot, and was aware that somebody was saying, 'Poor old Sid, he's right round the bend.' Sid was inclined to agree.

There were thousands of others throughout the land who could not bring themselves to listen to the Emperor – to whom he had himself referred as his innocent, suffering people – people like the teenage girl Yukie Tsuji, and fifteen-year-old Senzi Yamaguti, both of them still sightless from the A-bomb *pika* and tortured by the burns it had branded on their young bodies; people like Tadashi's sister, Saku, grieving over the loss of her three little girls – the eldest had died two days before. Saku's and Tadashi's parents did not hear the Emperor either; they were smitten by a strange malaise – high temperature, diarrhoea and vomiting blood, the unmistakable symptoms of a phenomenon now being widely reported among surviving victims and called 'atomic sickness'. Neither lived more than a few days. Tadashi himself had the same symptoms and felt too ill to pay attention to the Emperor's message. As for Sumiteru, prone on his stomach in the charnel house which had once been the elementary school at Isahaya, he vaguely heard the Emperor's voice, but its message never got past the fiery pain consuming his body.

Masato mourning his father; Yukie, Senzi, Saku, Tadashi and their parents, Sumiteru – they were but a few of the hundreds of thousands of innocent sheep sacrificed at the altar of Japanese militarism and mercilessly put to death or perpetual suffering by the US air-offensive.

The voice of the Crane was heard at the furthest limits of the defeated empire; in Korea one of those who listened, among a crowd of tearful school-children, was Eiko, the girl who, throughout the war, had kept on quietly with her studies, done her little bit for the war effort, and played on the beach at Seoul. She had never known the distress and the hardships suffered by the people of the homeland. But those cruel events were to catch up with her.

12

It was on the thirteenth, five days after the bomb, that Sumiteru's condition, static until then, suddenly became acute. His burnt flesh seemed to burst open; it began to bleed and felt as if it were on fire. Other than Ji-san's consoling words and his efforts to stem the bleeding with any rag he could find, there was no medical aid, not even first aid, available, either to Sumiteru or anyone else in that wretched place. Where children's laughter used to be heard, the foetid air was now heavy with the groans of the injured.

During those hot August days flies swarmed over them, laying eggs in the festering wounds which soon were crawling with maggots. Picking them out was the most revolting job assigned to the volunteer helpers. It proved to be dangerous too; many of them were contaminated by residual radiation emanating from the bodies of casualties and some died within a few days. There were no doctors available, no nurses – only volunteer workers who, devoted as they were, could provide no medicines, dressings or bandages, but only water and rice balls. Even with Ji-san helping, Sumiteru had difficulty getting food and drink into his mouth and swallowing it. His crushing load of pain made him less conscious of his other afflictions – high fever, diarrhoea stained with blood, and hair falling out in handfuls – all symptoms of 'atomic sickness'.

Sumiteru wondered why it had taken five days for his body to react and could only guess that most of its functions had been shocked into a temporary standstill. That was not surprising. The explosive force of the plutonium bomb dropped on Nagasaki was equivalent of some 23,000 times the high explosive (trinotrotoluene) in a 'conventional' bomb, and nearly twice as powerful as the Hiroshima uranium bomb. But the comparison with 'conventional' bombs is not as simple as that. An exploding atom bomb releases an enormous amount of radiant heat. The initial temperature at burst-point was several million degrees centigrade; with a conventional bomb it is some five thousand degrees centigrade. The explosion of an atom bomb creates devastating blast. The initial velocity of the A-bomb's shock wave exceeded by some three times the speed of sound, the pressure was equivalent to between seven and ten tons per square metre.

The crossroads on Route 206 where Sumiteru was hit was 1,800 metres from the hypocentre. Unshielded as he was by any buildings, the radiant heat which struck his back and arms would have been in the region of ten calories per square centimetre – a horrifying comparison with the 0.177 calories per square centimetre of the sun's radiant heat which warms the earth. A flash burn of some one thousand degrees centigrade flayed the skin off Sumiteru's body and caused burns to people as far as four kilometres from the burst-point. A wind of nearly 250 kilometres an hour, more violent than the worst of Japan's typhoons, had snatched him off his bicycle and thrown him to the ground at least ten paces away. It flung people against the walls of buildings, projecting them into the ruins, and hurled to their death those children who had waved to Sumiteru a second before the explosion.

An atom bomb releases a considerable amount of radio-activity. 'Initial radiation', within a minute of the explosion, consisted partly of alpha and beta particles. These are harmful to human and animal life when absorbed through the lungs or, in the form of irradiated food and drink, through the mouth. But the most lethal constituents of this 'ionizing radiation' were gamma rays and neutrons. The neutrons, on hitting the earth or road surfaces, and the tiles, bricks and concrete of buildings, were absorbed by these materials, which consequently became radioactive and continued to emit for some time dangerous amounts of 'residual radiation'.

Another source of radiation was the fall-out. Minute

radioactive particles were blown high into the atmosphere to be carried by the wind and to fall, heaven knew where or when, in the form of 'black rain' or dust, the 'ashes of death' – both of them radioactive.

Gamma rays and neutrons were harmful, or lethal, according to the dose, when the fell directly upon human beings or any other living thing. In humans they caused 'atomic sickness', or 'radiation sickness' which could kill within days or weeks or months and even after many years of unrelieved suffering. It had disastrous effects on unborn babies, whose mothers had been exposed to the bomb. It damaged the body's internal organs, causing genetic aberrations and diverse forms of cancer, as well as a permanent cancer psychosis among survivors, who feared and still do, as much for their progeny as for themselves.

Radiation spread its poisonous, invisible tentacles to the flora and fauna of the valley. It caused trees, bushes and flowers to wither. Where leaves were broad, as with camphor, taro and oleander, and roots went deep, the damage would be temporary, though some flowering bushes, like *Veronica persica*, would produce new flowers which were grotesquely deformed. All kinds of living creatures were smitten; the beautiful *mejiri* bird and ever-soaring kite were for some time no more to be seen on the hill unless half dead or divested of their feathers. Rainbow carp floated dead in ponds and rivers.

Only the insect community seemed to have weathered the searching, insidious rays of the atom bomb. Following its explosion, the air of Nagasaki reverberated no longer with the rhythmic beat of cicadas; they had evaporated in the holocaust. But cicadas spend a period of their life underground. Those lucky ones emerged in due course and set the air vibrating once more. Mosquitoes vanished for a few days, then returned in force. Earthworms, beetles and moths, hidden below ground or in convenient crevices, were unharmed. *Eurbellaria*, flat worms, lying on the bottom of ponds, also remained intact. If man were bent on self-extermination, it looked as if insects would inherit the earth.

Within two kilometres of the hypocentre, Nagasaki, once a fair city, was now, in her own flesh, contaminated by radio-activity which was transmitted as residual radiation to many of those who came searching for their missing relatives – the so-called 'early entrants'.

The maximum safe dose of radiation for workers on the Manhattan project had been fixed at 0.1 *Röntgen* a day or about thirty *Röntgen* or thirty *rads* a year. But the only realistic safe individual dose is what falls on the planet in the form of cosmic rays: twenty-five *milli-rads* a year. At 1,800 metres from the burst-point, Sumiteru, completely unshielded as he was, would have received on the surface of his body, in one shot, some forty *rads* of gamma rays and 0.3 *rads* of neutrons, well over the 'safe' *yearly* dose fixed for the Manhattan Project and more than 1,500 times the *yearly* dose from cosmic rays.

Such was the measure of the gigantic forces which had struck the small body of Sumiteru.

On the sixteenth, the day after the Emperor's proclamation, Ji-san told his grandson: 'Sumi-san, we are going to move you back to Nagayo.' Both Ji-san and Oba-chan had relatives living in the town, close by Michinoo, where Sumiteru had first set out on what was to be a series of painful, exhausting journeys in search of proper medical care. With the help of two voluntary workers Ji-san lifted Sumiteru and laid him on his stomach in a rear-cart, a solid wooden barrow with two iron-tyred wheels and no springs. Ji-san and the two volunteers pulled him over the paved streets as far as the station where they transferred him into the Nagayo train, which was nearly empty; a great human current was flowing out of Nagasaki but few were making their way towards the stricken city.

At Nagayo, the relatives were at the station, with rice balls and sympathy, but neither could assuage Sumiteru's agony during the three-kilometre journey, again by rear-cart, to the elementary school, now converted into a temporary hospital.

It was here, for the first time since the bomb had exploded a week before, that Sumiteru met a professional doctor. The medical treatment which Ji-san's relatives had assured him was available was forthwith administered. He had been laid, as before, on a *tatami* on the floor. The doctor and his team of two men from Hario naval base were woefully short of medicine. For Sumiteru, they concocted their own. They took paper and burnt it to ashes. Sumiteru could not see them, but the smell was unmistakable. He did watch, however, as they milled the ashes into a powder which they then stirred into maize oil, after which they proceeded to dab the strange mixture all over Sumiteru's wounds – on top of the engine-oil which had been there for a week. The pain that this crude operation caused him was so unbearable that each day, when the doctors came, he pleaded with them: 'No, it hurts too much; kill me instead, kill me! I want to die.' Death, he was sure, would be preferable, to lying there flat on his stomach hardly able to breath or eat or sleep for the racking pain. 'Let me die!' he begged them.

If Sumiteru no longer felt either the desire or the will to live, his wiry little body, despite its cruel wounds, seemed to be holding out on its own. In mid-September, Sumiteru was extricated from the hellish torture chamber of Nagayo and moved to the emergency hospital set up in Nagasaki, at Shinkozen primary school, just opposite the main post office which, in his happy days as a postman, had been something of a second home. This time he travelled the whole way from Nagayo lying in a rear-cart drawn by Ji-san and two of his relatives. Another man walked alongside with an umbrella, shading Sumiteru from the hot September sun. Fourteen kilometres they walked, with the rear-cart bumping over the pitted surface of Route 206; at each bump Sumiteru felt as if he had been stabbed with a long knife. But he was glad that his escort were countrymen; their pace was fast and in less than four hours Sumiteru was at the Shinkozen hospital, being laid, for a change, on a bed.

This unaccustomed comfort was to do nothing to ease his suffering, any more than was the excellent medical care available. By now, experienced medical teams had moved in. One was made up from the survivors of Nagasaki Medical University; others came from universities and medical schools all over Japan, a few from the naval bases on Kyushu Island. Medical supplies were being rushed in by the International Red Cross, the American Red Cross and US Army. During the weeks that followed the bomb, thousands had died through want of proper medical treatment. Now, things were getting organized, and men, erstwhile enemies, were beginning once more to behave towards each other in a civilized way.

Sumiteru realized immediately that he was now in competent, professional hands. He received penicillin injections and a blood transfusion. But his body must have been too damaged internally by radiation, for it would not take the fresh blood. His condition did not improve as he lay, day in, day out, on his stomach, in ceaseless pain, always longing for the end. Like the rest of the patients, he was treated by the overworked hospital staff as an inanimate object, without any particular sympathy or tenderness. That was normal. One day, two US medical corps men came and stood over him; without a word or gesture of pity, they took flashlight photographs of his ugly, suppurating wounds. Neither the coldness of the hospital staff nor the callousness of the Americans meant anything to him. Ji-san, the faithful Ji-san, was always there. It was he who possessed the will for Sumiteru to live, which was lacking in the boy himself.

Shinkozen was another hell, a more sophisticated one than Nagayo, but a hell none the less of bodily pain and spiritual desolation. Sumiteru blamed no one; the hell was within him, his private hell.

With no sign of his wounds healing, it was decided to move him to Omura naval hospital, near Isahaya, which was better adapted to long-term treatment – at least for patients who survived long enough. Many did not. The hospital was permanently overcrowded with the most serious atom-bomb cases; but the death-rate being high, the mournful process of evacuating the dead and replacing them with the half-dead, eventually brought Sumiteru his turn. An ambulance took him and Ji-san to Nagasaki station where the railway track had been temporarily relaid. The train took them back up the valley, still desolate and lifeless, past Michinoo and Nagayo and on about half a dozen kilometres beyond Isahaya to Omura where they were driven by truck to the naval hospital, a group of thirteen solid two-storey wooden blocks. Sumiteru was installed in Block 6. Once again his mutilated body was stretched face downwards on a long bed; he was to remain in that position for another eighteen months. Such an awful prospect was far from his own thoughts. He was bent on dying and so being spared from his ceaseless torture.

Sumiteru was placed in the care of Doctor Matsuo, a small, bespectacled man, in a white coat. The doctor patiently tried out a variety of ointments on Sumiteru's wounds, covering them with gauze, but none had the slightest effect, save to provoke the pitiful, invariable cry from Sumiteru: 'It hurts too much. I can't bear it. Kill me! Please let me die!' The doctor persisted, trying out more and more different dressings. Meanwhile he had given Sumiteru a perfusion which, drop by drop, fed pain killer and nourishment into the boy's body and kept him alive. Sumiteru, lying face downward, had little success with his own attempts to feed himself with chopsticks. He had to raise his head and this interfered with his swallowing. Once he choked and, half suffocating, passed out. Doctor Matsuo clamped a forceps on to his patient's tongue to prevent him from swallowing it. In his weak state, it was surprising that Sumiteru did not go under for the last time. Slowly, however, he recovered consciousness and as he did so there came back to him the unmistakable urge to hold on, to survive. It was not to last for long.

Teiji and Keiko came regularly to see their younger brother. 'Hold on,' they would tell him. 'You are getting better.' Sumiteru, though grateful, was not convinced. Oba-chan's visits were more rare and, unable to bear the sight of her Sumi-chan's great affliction, she never stayed long. One day, an unexpected visitor turned up: Sadamachi, Sumiteru's father, who, when his wife died sixteen years before, had abandoned his young family to Oba-chan. Sumiteru was then too young to have known his father, though Sadamachi still remembered the soft-skinned baby he used to hold in his arms. Years had passed and now there remained nothing between father and son, but Sadamachi, with the image of the infant still in mind, was so overcome at the sight of Sumiteru's shattered body that he could only bow, mumble a few words and hurry from the ward. Sumiteru felt grateful for his father's visit, yet he could not find it in himself to thank him. He was always pleased to see Oba-chan, Keiko and Teiji, for he felt close to them and they helped to lift him up out of the black abyss of despair into which he had fallen. But as soon as his family were gone and he was alone again with himself, he sank back once more into the dark, longing for death to end the unbearable pain of being alive.

Following a visit in March 1946, the family foregathered at Oba-chan's house. They talked long of Sumiteru and his chances of recovery. None of them, not even Ji-san, believed he could live more than a few days. They decided to make arrangements for his funeral.

13

Seven months had gone by since Ji-san had found Sumiteru lying half-dead in the shade of a tall tree at Michinoo station. At the same station, not long afterwards, there arrived a fifteen-year-old schoolgirl, Eiko, the one who had spent the war with her parents and twin sister in Seoul. Her parents stayed behind for the time being to put their affairs in order, while Eiko and her twin sister Shizuko were sent off in the care of relatives by train to Pusan, the port in the south of Korea. It was only after several days in that big city that they managed to find a boat bound for Japan. It landed them three days later at Shimonozeki, close to Kokura, that city in the north of Kyushu which the clouds had protected from the second A-bomb.

At Shimonozeki the landing formalities were controlled by the American Army. Eiko had heard, like everyone else, that the US soldiers were bent on revenge, so she felt afraid. Her fears were quickly dispelled when she saw that the GIs behaved just like any other officials she had ever met, except in one respect: they methodically removed the watches from each passenger's wrist. That really upset her; Eiko's watch was a present from her father – the only man, so far, in her life.

That night the passengers were lodged in a camp; it was there that Eiko heard for the first time that Nagasaki had been hit by an atom bomb, though she did not quite understand what that was. Next day she and her sister found a train to take them the 180-odd kilometres to her father's home in Noda, a hamlet at Togitsu, a fishing village beyond the top of the Nagasaki valley. The local station was Michinoo. Just over three hours later the train steamed into Michinoo station. Eiko noticed that there was no glass in the windows of the small half-timbered building. Michinoo station was more than three kilometres from the hypocentre; it would be months before glass would be available to replace the windows shattered on 9 August. Eiko and her sister walked out of the station and waited in the shade of a tall tree nearby – the one beneath which Sumiteru had lain. Soon a cart drawn by two ambling bullocks rumbled up to the station. Driving it was their uncle, their father's brother, whom they greeted with bows and smiles and rapid exchanges of family news. As they chatted, one thing quickly became clear to Eiko: the times ahead were not going to be so easy as those spent in their suburban house in Seoul.

It took them about an hour – but for the luggage it would have been quicker to walk – to cover the two kilometres or so to their grandparents' home in Noda, where more bows and smiles and greetings were exchanged. The family, or at least the vanguard, had come home. Eiko's parents arrived the following month.

Times were indeed hard, mainly because of a serious short-age of food. Wise man that he was, Eiko's father had sent money home from Korea to his family. With it, they had bought a *taan* of farming land – about a thousand square metres or a quarter of an acre. That would at least be enough to keep the family provided – given the labour. This was to be supplied by Eiko who, though still weak from malaria con-tracted in Korea, uncomplainingly made the abrupt change from suburban Seoul and the beach at Ginse to toiling on the land at Noda. She found it very hard at first but that charming little place had its consolations. Off the beaten track, it lay in a broad dip of the land formed by the surrounding green moun-tains. *No* means 'green field', *da* 'rice field': 'The place of green rice fields' – that was Noda. Every day, Eiko was up at sun-rise and after a breakfast of boiled rice with *misoshuru* – soya bean sauce – and pickles, she walked over to the plot. It was for the most part planted with rice, with some space left for eggplants, potatoes and beans. It was the first time in her life that Eiko had ever done serious manual work, but she had no choice: there was no one else available to work the land.

Eiko worked so hard that she had little time for anything else. She was too young to go out alone with a boy friend – even if she had had one. But Eiko, whether she was working on the land or as a pupil at the Togitsu Youth School, had no time for boy friends. Nagasaki, just over the hill, was for her another world. She had heard that many Togitsu commuters had been lost in the Nagasaki disaster; people had gone into Nagasaki looking for relatives. A few were able to bring them back home; others, after a fruitless search, had brought back anything useful they could find among the ruins, yet others returned with nothing but the deadly symptoms of radiation sickness. To Eiko, Nagasaki seemed a sinister place which she had no wish to visit.

But one autumn day Eiko did go to Nagasaki; with her went Yoshie, her brother Masami's widow. In a sense their mission was the same as that of the 'early entrants' after the bomb – to look for their relatives. Only it was the ashes of Masami in an urn, and those of his brother Tetumi in another, that the two girls went to fetch at the Go-shinzi Buddhist temple, at the bottom of the hill below Oba-chan's home.

The Japanese Government, though it had never informed the family of Masami's and Tetumi's death in action had, in its benevolence, returned to the family the ashes of each one in an urn. But were the contents of the urns really the ashes of those two loved ones? Yoshie did not believe so, neither did Eiko. But they came home with the urns, and at the local Buddhist temple in Togitsu, before the gathered family, the urns were buried in one grave marked by two headstones – 'Masami, killed in action'; 'Tetumi, killed in action.'

Eiko was glad to go back to the fields of Noda. The rice had been gathered in and winnowed; the oranges picked from the trees and the persimmons were ripening to an orange pink. Giant, gorgeously coloured butterflies floated on the heavy warm air which vibrated with the ceaseless strumming of cicadas – the kind which sound more like a bird. It was time, the Japanese say, to pluck the fruit from the persimmon tree.

14

Just beyond the window of his ward in Block 6 of the Omura naval hospital, Sumiteru too had noticed a tall persimmon tree. As he lay gazing at it, memories came back to him from the past: the fun he used to have with Teiji on the hill, hunting birds and rabbits, hide-and-seek, cross-country races with his school-mates, climbing trees. The persimmon was one of his favourite trees, only one had to be careful, for the branches broke easily. He remembered how Oba-chan would scold him for returning late and chase him with a broom, and how he would shin up the nearest tree to escape her wrath. But Oba-chan was good; it was thanks to her that he had spent such a happy childhood on the hill. He let his thoughts run on; those had been lovely days, and so, in a different way, were the days he had spent as a postman. They were great days too, speeding on the red bicycle, the feeling of flying, friends at every stop.

The pleasant visions faded and Sumiteru's thoughts came back to the stark present, to the hospital bed on which he lay. He kept on looking through the window at the persimmon tree. On the hill above the torpedo factory such a tree had given him some meagre succour; the persimmon would always be his special tree, even though it meant to him both joy and sorrow — the memories of a happy childhood which turned into the nightmare of which he was now a wretched prisoner.

Looking at the persimmon, Sumiteru felt more and more miserable. Not only was he not recovering, he was actually getting worse. Bedsores on his cheeks, his chest and knees aggravated the already unbearable torture: anaemia was weakening him and making him wonder if his blood-forming functions had been permanently damaged by radiation. The penicillin and all the other antiseptic treatments he had been receiving for months were no longer effective. His back became septic again. A new summer was not far off and the warmer weather brought flies swarming into the ward. Like all the patients, Sumiteru lay under a mosquito net, but still the flies got in. As at Isahaya the previous autumn, they laid their eggs in the raw flesh of his back, which was soon teeming with a loathsome mass of white maggots. Pus oozed from his back, streamed down his sides and collected in his bed. He felt he was lying in a sea of pus. The stink of it revolted him, and Sumiteru now cried out more insistently than ever: 'Kill me, kill me; let me die!'

Lying in that purulent mess, his mind was tormented by a single theme, 'the stink of man's rottenness'. Though in no way to blame for the vileness of his own body, once so strong and athletic, he was now repelled by its weakness and immobility. Before the bomb he had been clean; the bomb had defiled him. Whose fault was it? The Americans, he reasoned, could not be held to blame in the first place. Japan, as far as he knew, had started the war. He remembered how his teacher, following the propaganda line, had kept insisting that Japan must win; he recalled the delirious public rejoicings as victory followed victory. It was against the militarists who had led Japan into war and to ultimate, miserable defeat that Sumiteru felt bitter revolt. They were the first to blame for the calamity which had befallen Japan. It was they who exemplified 'the stink of man's rottenness'. They had callously sacrificed the civilian population for their own ends. It sickened him to think that young people like himself should have had to bear such atrocious sufferings on the militarists' behalf.

The atom bomb was a crime against humanity; if the Americans had dropped it, the Japanese military had provoked it; they were the ones primarily responsible. For the first time in his life, Sumiteru felt hatred boiling inside him – hatred for war, for the militarist clique and the profiteers, who thrived on war. He longed all the more for death to take him away, out of this stinking, rotten world.

The thought that he was permanently harmed filled him with chagrin. The happy days were over, gone for ever. At his age, sixteen, it looked as if pain and sorrow were to be his lot for the rest of his life – if indeed he was going to live. All the time he wondered: am I going to survive or am I dying? Ji-san's presence was a comfort, but his words of encouragement meant no more now to Sumiteru; the fight had gone clean out of him. He felt that death was close and willingly let himself drift on down towards the end.

One morning in October 1946 Doctor Matsuo came into the ward accompanied by another man in white. They approached the prone, inert body of Sumiteru, and Doctor Matsuo, bending over him, said: 'This is Doctor Takita. He comes from Kumamoto Medical University and has brought a new medicine for you.' Doctor Matsuo did not dare to add anything about his hopes for the new medicine; there had been so many failures in the past.

The product was different to all those that Sumiteru had received so far, which, as ointments or lotions, had been applied externally on his wounds. The new treatment consisted of two products which had to be swallowed: a green-coloured pill called *Koha* and a white powder, *Shiko*. Doctor Matsuo started Sumiteru off on *Koha*, two pills a day, which he allowed to dissolve on his tongue and then swallowed. At the end of a week Sumiteru felt in less pain. Hardly daring to admit it, he told the Doctor that he was feeling better. He was then taken off *Koha* and put on to *Shiko*. But the white powder lacked the magic qualities of the green pill, *Koha*. To his utter dismay, Sumiteru felt himself relapsing into the hell from which *Koha* had given hope of raising him.

He was put back again on to *Koha* and after a day or two he sensed he was once again on the upward climb. Gradually the fight came back into him until he felt determined to make a final bid for his life. Only one thing worried him: would his back, ravaged by burns, suppurating and eaten by maggots, ever heal completely?

When, one day early in 1947, he told Doctor Matsuo of his

doubts the doctor went and fetched a large mirror. Holding it so that Sumiteru could see his back, he said: 'Take a look and see how well your back is doing.' Sumiteru, twisting his head from one extreme to the other, was able, for the first time, to see what the atom bomb had done to him. He was shocked at the extent of the burn, which covered his entire back, but over it had formed, like shiny parchment, a thin layer of skin, flawless save for one open sore in the lower spinal region. Sumiteru was convinced. He was also pleased to see that his hair had grown again, thick, black and shiny. He was on the mend, but it would take time.

The early months of 1947 passed and Sumiteru, still lying on his stomach, would every day exercise his legs, kicking them in the air, preparing for the great moment when he would again stand on his own feet. It happened one day in May. With the doctor, Ji-san and a small crowd of patients watching tensely, as if he were an infant taking his first few paces, Sumiteru wriggled, still face down, until his feet and legs hung over the side of the bed. Then, holding on to it, he transferred his weight to his feet and slowly straightened himself until he stood up. As somebody handed him a pair of crutches, he was thinking: I have crawled up at last out of hell. I really am alive again. A little burst of applause from those watching surprised him. He bowed gratefully, then moved unobtrusively to where Ji-san was standing. Smiling, he made a bow to his grandfather and said: 'Thank you, Ji-san, it is really you who have saved me.'

What surprised Sumiteru most was to feel so tall. In the twenty-one months that he had been lying face down he had grown some thirty centimetres. Without realizing it, he had developed from a mite into a young man.

Sumiteru was eighteen and a half. What should have been the best years of his youth had been spent in hell, and there were still many months of hospital confinement ahead. The prospect did not dismay him too much; after a week, he was walking without crutches and so elated at having won his fight for survival that he would leave the future to take care of itself. He knew all the same that there were more trials to come.

For one thing, though his massive burns were superficially healed, time would be needed before their condition became stable – that wound in his back, still open and suppurating, had to be dressed daily. The burns on his left arm, though they healed faster, developed keloid, an overgrowth of skin tissue which prevented the elbow joint from extending fully. A year later, in 1948, the doctors decided on surgery. A graft was made with skin from Sumiteru's right thigh. It took, but did not improve the movement of the arm which, for the rest of Sumiteru's life, would remain half useless.

From talking to Doctor Matsuo and the patients in his ward he had learnt a little about radiation – enough to convince himself that he had received a heavy dose. He had experienced the ordeal of radiation sickness – falling hair, bloody diarrhoea, fever, vomiting. Radiation had apparently injured his blood cells, reaching down to the bone-marrow where blood cells are produced and so impairing the healing of his burns.

Not long after the arm operation, Sumiteru was once more called to the surgery; this time for a sternum puncture, a painful stab in the chest with a thick needle to extract bone-marrow for examination. This test proved to the doctors that the production of blood cells in his body was abnormally low. They told Sumiteru nothing, which suggested to him that all was not well. That did not worry him too much; he could now stand up and walk around without crutches. Though he had to stay on for many months under observation in Omura hospital, Sumiteru did not for an instant doubt that his battle was won.

He had gained something of a reputation among the staff and patients, and on the day of his departure in March 1949 they all turned out to bid him farewell. In a smart blue suit (borrowed from Teiji) and carrying his few effects wrapped in a *furoshiki*, he walked away with cries of *sayonara* sounding in his ears, and kept on walking until he was beyond earshot, consciously resisting the temptation to turn back for a last look at his friends and the hospital. For all that the hospital represented in the way of professional care and human sympathy, to Sumiteru it meant, much more vividly, a long and agonizing battle against death, a wearisome, almost impossible climb up out of hell to a sane and normal existence. Sumiteru had escaped from death; the main battle for survival was behind him. He would now have to set his face towards the future and remake his life, shattered as it had been at the beginning of his manhood.

From Omura he took the train – the one that had brought him there, so long ago it seemed, in which he had been dumped face downwards on a board, among a heap of groaning, bleeding bodies. Now he sat comfortably staring out of the window. Nothing had changed in that fertile countryside. It was the towns, not the country, which had been ravaged by war. The train stopped in turn at Isahaya, Nagayo and Michinoo. At Michinoo, Sumiteru noticed the tree beneath which Ji-san had found him, half-dead. All those places held for him morbid memories, and he tried not to think of them.

As the train rattled on down the valley, he realized that Nagasaki was no longer the desert of charred and shattered buildings he had left nearly four years before. The city was beginning to rise out of the ashes; it was coming to life again. From the train he could see new houses and buildings going up. The people of Nagasaki had begun the redoubtable task of rebuilding their desecrated city.

But many of the wounds left by the atom bomb were still far from healed and the Japanese Government were slow to compensate the victims. Hundreds of people whom the bomb had dispossessed of their home, their chattels and, all too often, their family, were living in shacks huddled together down by the riverside. Sumiteru, who had so often passed that way on his red bicycle, was shocked to see such a sordid slum. A little further, clinging precariously to the fire-scarred hillside opposite, he could see another shanty town. There, more of the atom bomb's miserable victims eked out a useless, humiliating existence, crammed, a dozen or so together, into each of the bamboo hovels. The place was called the Ant City. Its denizens suffered both from their squalid quarters and from the contempt of the community, which fell with particular harshness on their children; ostracized for living in Ant City, they were left to trail the rest of the class. Christian missions – Jesuit, Franciscan and Augustinian – cared for these poor people until at last the authorities took over.

Through the carriage window Sumiteru looked out sadly on their miserable dwellings. But it was pointless to compare their sufferings with his own; his had been grievous enough and he well knew that he would have to endure their consequences for the rest of his life.

Sumiteru got off the train at Nagasaki station and from there walked to the Ohato pier where he took the ferry to the Asahi pier on the other side of the harbour. How often had he made that crossing – but so much had changed in his own life and the city's since the last time, that day in August 1945. Looking up the valley he could see none of the old familiar landmarks – Mitsubishi Electric, Mitsubishi Steel and the rest. New buildings were rising in their place.

From the Asahi pier he began the steep ascent to Oba-chan's house. It was harder going now, after all he had been through and when he came to a flight of steps he would sit for a moment and take a breather. At last he arrived at Oba-chan's house – his house, in a way, because it was so dear to him. His grandmother and Ji-san were waiting for him. Sumiteru bowed to them, in the way of the Japanese, slipped off his shoes and entered the house. He had come home at last.

15

That evening they ate a typical celebration meal: raw fish with soya beans and rice coloured with the juice of *azuki*, red beans. They talked cheerfully and toasted Sumiteru's return with *sake*. During the next ten days Sumiteru had time to take stock of his surroundings, of his past and the problems it would create for him in the future. The old house was the same, its missing tiles replaced and its shattered windows mended – though only recently, because of the shortage of glass. The hill, with its woods and open spaces, that Sumiteru had always considered his own playground, the slope where the path and the 150 steps went down towards the Mitsubishi shipyard, and the western slopes which rolled away valley after valley to the sea, were, too, the same as ever. His thoughts went back to the happy times he had spent on the hill and it gladdened him to see it still looking so beautiful.

But the hills which bounded the Urakami valley – he could take in much more now than from the train – had been defaced by the atom bomb. They were no longer green with wild plants and pines; the bomb's thermal rays had charred them almost to the skyline. Bamboo trees as far as six kilometres from the burst-point were scorched; needle-leaved trees like the cedar and the pine had proved particularly sensitive to radioactivity. Wooded areas not blackened by fire were sallowed a yellowish-brown by ionizing radiation and had eventually withered and died.

Behind the house, Sumiteru could see that Inasa, Nagasaki's sacred hill, had been ravaged to within a hundred metres of its summit. It sickened him to see how the hills, once a luxuriant green, had been so wantonly laid waste, but he did not doubt that man and nature between them would contrive in time to repair these ugly, gigantic scars and cover them with a new mantle of green.

Since the atomic bomb, men in Nagasaki had already done much to put things back in order. One of them was a young Japanese doctor, Takashi Nagai, a Christian by faith and a radiologist by profession. When the bomb demolished the University hospital where he was working he was one of the few survivors; he later discovered the ashes of his wife, Midori, in their gutted home. The doctor himself was already contaminated by radiation through his professional work.

When word spread that the soil of Nagasaki would remain radioactive for another seventy-five years, Nagai walked round with his geiger counter and pronounced it clean. On hands and knees he searched among the ruins of Urakami cathedral for its famous bell. He found it; had it re-hung and set tolling again. Inspired by his books and poems, readers the world over sent him funds, some of which he used to replace the flowers, shrubs and cherry trees devastated by the bomb. He thought of children, his own and everybody else's who would in future people the world. He had a school built and through his teachings and writings warned the young against the madness of war and violence. By 1948 it was clear that radiation had done its sinister work; Nagai's days were numbered. When, in 1951, he died, he was only forty-three.

In Nagasaki and far beyond, Nagai was hailed as a saint and a martyr. His example left a deep impression on Sumiteru, who felt more determined than ever, his infirmity notwithstanding, to make the most of his life as long as it lasted. How long that would be was uncertain, for Sumiteru was one of those few hundred thousand in Hiroshima and Nagasaki who had suffered – and survived – a unique experience. Never before had destruction so sudden and complete been visited upon man. The sheer horror of the *pika-don*, the single, blinding flash and unearthly thunder, the raging hot wind of the blast, would be for ever imprinted on the survivors' minds and on their bodies too. The mighty, instantaneous shock had arrested their psychological functions, deprived them of their humanity. They felt as if imprisoned in a vacuum, surrounded by emptiness. The 'death saturation', the multitudes around them who had perished, left them with the feeling that they, too, should have died. Survival seemed to them unnatural, culpable even, in a situation where death and desolation reigned, where the abrupt collapse of order and existence had caused a total disintegration of society. With most of them all desire to live had vanished. They would rather have joined the great host of departed spirits than gone on living on this cursed earth.

Sumiteru's experience, it is true, was different from that of the majority. Firstly, he discovered in himself, in the immediate aftermath of the explosion, an extraordinary, inflexible will to survive – an animal instinct which life on the hill had strongly awakened in him. Certainly, when his suffering became intolerable, the will to live departed from him – he longed to quit this earth and all its pain and horror – but when, after seemingly interminable suffering, his body began to heal, his mind, too, took part in the process. Time was needed. Hard as it had been for Sumiteru to endure nearly four years of hospital, he had benefited, at least during the last two years, from living in a small world apart where all were survivors – and on the mend. Together, they created an atmosphere of solidarity where the ruling principles were no longer death and desolation, but life and hope.

Now he was home again and back in the current of everyday life, Sumiteru, with these principles firmly in mind, faced the future. It was a precarious one, to say the least. He would have to live for the rest of his life under the threat of delayed radiation effects. If ever he had children, nobody would know for certain whether they too, and their offspring for generations to come, might not be affected – deformed or mentally retarded. If delayed radiation effects should ever prevent him from playing his role as the bread-winner, or, worse, cause his premature death, his family would suffer. Finally, there was the prospect, by no means negligible, of discrimination against him and his children on the grounds of his being an A-bomb victim. The spectre of death and desolation, though it could be held at a distance, would inevitably haunt Sumiteru and every other A-bomb victim for the rest of their lives.

Sumiteru was aware that he would have to live with all these uncertainties. That did not deter him. He had won his fight for life; now he was resolved to function as well as any normal man.

16

His problems began from the moment of his return. When he reported to his old chief at the main post office on 1 April he could not rid himself of a feeling of self-consciousness about his scars. It was still early in the year and his winter clothes hid all but the ugly bed-sore on his face and the burns on his hands. But when summer came, the time for short sleeves and swimming with his friends, would he have the courage to face them with such a sorely disfigured body?

His fears were calmed, if not entirely dispelled, that morning. His chief greeted him warmly, so did his old friends, though many were missing, victims of the catastrophe from which he had so barely escaped. As a survivor, his colleagues showed him particular sympathy. 'Sumiteru-san', the chief told him, 'we all know what a bad time you've been through and we're proud you have come back to join us.' Sumiteru had already, a few days earlier, been down to see the clerk to sign for his re-engagement. Now the chief told him: 'I'm giving you a job which I hope will not take too much out of you. Telegram deliveries. You won't serve any particular district, but deliver all over the city. And as we're no longer at war, thank God, I shan't expect you to get from here to the Sumiyoshi-machi – it's been promoted from a *cho* – in fifteen minutes. Remember? You used to be the champion, but now I want you to take it more easily. Don't bust yourself. We want you to stay with us.' As Sumiteru turned to go, the chief called after him: 'One last word, Sumiteru-san. You know the Americans are still in occupation. They destroyed our city – for that you either forgive them or you don't. I don't – so many of my family were killed. We were all told that they were going to butcher us, rape our women and so on, but they've behaved well on the whole. Show them a proper respect and you'll have no trouble.'

Sumiteru bowed and left. As he walked back towards the Ohato pier he reflected on what the chief had said. It was not the bit about the Americans which stuck in his mind, but what he had said about taking it easy, 'Don't bust yourself or try to get to Sumiyoshi-machi in fifteen minutes.' As he slowly climbed the path and the 150 steps up from the Asahi pier to Oba-chan's, the question which was bothering him was: Am I up to the job? Shall I ever make it?

During the days that followed, Sumiteru, on a brand new red bicycle, began to rediscover Nagasaki – and himself. The city he had last seen in ruins was now rapidly taking shape again – albeit a changed one. He found his way without any trouble through the streets, which had nearly all been restored along the lines of the original ones. Some of them, like Route 206, were now wider and replanted down each side with sapling trees – more often than not with Nagasaki's symbolic tree the *Nan-Kin haze*, the Chinese tallow tree, and the *Sakura*, the pink-blossomed cherry. Work had begun on the public parks and gardens where the city flower, *Ajisahi*, the hydrangea, was pushing out its early shoots.

The main reconstruction work was taking place downtown, in the old city, but as far up the valley as Sumiyoshi-machi, Sumiteru's old beat, a number of new buildings were going up. One of them was the international Cultural Hall, another the sub-post office. Down-town business in the shops was now more or less as usual, though in front of the railway station it was still slow. The port was as busy as ever; across the harbour new ships were building in the Mitsubishi yard and at the quay upstream the trawlers of the fishing fleet were ceaselessly coming and going. Despite its remaining scars, Nagasaki was unmistakably being raised from the dead.

All these things, and many more, Sumiteru noticed as he pedalled round the city. If his new beat was considerably larger, the tempo was slower. He found to his delight that he had lost little, if any of his old dash, his love of speed – or at least the sensation of speed, and the rush of air against his face, which made him feel as if he were flying. But when the time came for him to knock off, to range his shining red bicycle alongside the others, he could not deny that he felt worn out – and he still had to walk down to the Ohato pier, take the ferry to the other side and climb the steep path home. By then he was utterly exhausted.

At night, before falling asleep, Sumiteru would turn the situation over in his mind. While he knew that the spirit was more than willing, the flesh, through no fault of his own, was weaker than he would have wished. That worried him, for he could do nothing about it, save to refuse to give in to the failings of his body. He must drive it on, make it achieve what he willed. And that, essentially, was to fight against defeatism, against falling back into the 'death and desolation' mentality he had known during those hellish months in Omura hospital. Every A-bomb survivor in his own way had to fight the same fight with more or less success. Sumiteru's way was to keep pedalling, eight hours a day, delivering telegrams, then to walk back home, recover his strength and get on with the same job next day. He accepted the challenge quite calmly.

Regularly every two months he reported to the surgery department at the University hospital for a blood test. The result was always the same – positive. The doctors made no secret of the fact that Sumiteru was still suffering from the delayed effects of radiation; his body's blood-forming functions were inadequate, his white and red blood cell count was below normal; so were the platelets, which play a role in blood coagulation. That explained his continuing fatigue. He must be patient, they told him, things should get better in time. He was given injections to help his recovery.

These dubious prognostications did not worry Sumiteru too much. They seemed minor compared with all the pains and horrors he had already endured. The one thing that really mattered was to get on with his job – otherwise he would lose it, and that would be worse than any passing medical problem.

One such did crop up in 1951 – it arose not from his blood,

but from his burns and from two bed-sores, among the many on other parts of his body which had tortured him during those months of lying face downwards in hospital. These two, on his left cheek, had refused to heal. He had always been self-conscious about them, the more so because, though men affected not to notice them, women were clearly embarrassed. The same was true of an overgrowth of scar tissue, on the burnt skin of his left ear. The celebrated Professor Shirabe, of the University hospital, skilfully dissimulated all these ugly wounds by plastic surgery. After a few days, Sumiteru was back at his job and feeling reassured.

17

A-bomb survivors were extremely vulnerable in a society which tended to regard them as a people apart; tainted by the atom bomb and its effects – disfiguring burns, psychological problems and radiation sickness; tainted by death itself. More and more they met together to talk, not so much about their past experiences, as about the consequences of the bomb on their daily lives. In the minds of many of them there still remained an inkling of that complex called 'death guilt', a sense of shame at having survived mass extermination. Why had they not died with the rest? The thought obsessed many of them.

The survivors sought another explanation. What was the meaning of that mass sacrifice of innocents, of their kith and kin, of their close friends? The short answer was that they had died in the cause of Japan's ultimate victory. But there had been no victory, only defeat and ignominious surrender. Besides, the Emperor in his proclamation to the nation had talked of the folly of continuing the war; surrender, he had said, was the proper course. So the sacrifice had been completely in vain.

When in September 1945 the American occupation forces took over, their GHQ began to put across a different rationale. The sacrifices by the victims of American air-raids were not made for the honour and glory of Japan. The real meaning of their sacrifice was that it enabled the Japanese people to rid themselves of the wicked militarist government. But why, wondered simple, honest people, why go for us civilians and not the military themselves?

So civilian air-raid survivors were now expected to believe, after the gospel according to the Americans, that their sacrifice and that of the dead, had brought democracy and peace to Japan. This explanation held good as much for the victims of 'conventional' bombing – with high explosive and napalm – as for those of the atomic bomb. It was blithely claimed – and still is – that 'conventional' air-raids and A-bomb raids are analogous. So they may have been in terms of aggregate carnage and material destruction. But there was an essential difference between atomic and conventional bombs. The A-bomb represented, for those times, the ultimate in what the military manuals call 'economy of force': one bomb, one bomber aircraft and one second to demolish a whole city and kill or maim most of its inhabitants. The A-bomb's thermal rays were incalculably more destructive than napalm, its single blast more devastating than thousands of tons of TNT ('conventional') bombs. Finally, radioactivity – unique to the A-bomb – killed some people quickly but brought to others a long, lingering death and yet others lasting suffering and anxiety. The A-bomb was by far the most evil, cruel and efficacious weapon ever devised by man.

During the few weeks before the American occupying force had established its authority in Japan, Japanese doctors and scientists, journalists and photographers, were able to gather a certain amount of invaluable information about the atom bombs. But four weeks after the Nagasaki bomb, American GHQ issued a callous statement to the effect that people likely to die from radiation sickness were simply to be left to die. They were not considered worth saving. The US occupation authorities did everything possible to play down the effects of the A-bomb. A press directive in September imposed censorship on radio broadcasts and the printed media. Details of the death and desolation caused by the A-bombs were henceforth unmentionable as were medical reports on the treatment of victims. Anti-nuclear demonstrations also, were naturally forbidden. American GHQ, on the other hand, welcomed articles praising the A-bomb's unprecedented power and efficacy.

Late in November 1945 further GHQ directives declared that Japanese doctors, scientists and sociologists were forbidden to undertake any medical or scientific research on the bomb or its effects without permission. Were they allowed, exceptionally, to do so, the publication of their reports was prohibited.

The four years which followed the raids on Hiroshima and Nagasaki left the Americans with a world monopoly of the A-bomb. Then, in 1949, Stalin's urgent order on the morrow of Hiroshima was finally executed; the Soviets successfully exploded their first atomic device. In Japan, American preaching on atomic weapons once more changed – to the accompaniment of the thunder of further A-bomb tests including, in 1952, one by Britain. The new US line was that nuclear weapons, piles of them, were essential not only to win wars, as in the past, but to prevent them happening in the future. The atom bomb had replaced the cooing dove as the harbinger of peace.

At that, the Japanese A-bomb survivors rose in protest. They, after all, were the only people on earth who knew what they were talking about when it came to being on the receiving end of a nuclear bomb. Far from being a symbol of peace, they reasoned, the atom bomb was the negation of all life on earth – human, animal and plant. Those victims who, to their lasting cost, had survived the A-bomb, would never approve the further use of nuclear weapons.

As long as the US occupation authority continued to impose restrictions on the Japanese in the fields of nuclear research and anti-nuclear demonstrations, the Japanese remained frustrated in their determination to establish that the A-bomb was inadmissible as a weapon of war. The Americans prevented Japanese delegates from attending the first World Assembly to Protect the Peace, held in 1949 in Paris and Prague, which called for an absolute ban on nuclear weapons. A year later, in May 1950, in its famous Stockholm appeal, the World Assembly roundly declared that any nation starting a nuclear war would be held guilty of a crime against humanity.

Nevertheless, when the Korean war started the following month, President Truman made it clear that the atomic bomb could be used. France and Britain protested, but more effective, probably, was the growing world opinion that deterred Truman from another atomic massacre.

The Stockholm Appeal was warmly supported in Hiroshima and Nagasaki, but with the outbreak of the Korean war, the United States officially suppressed all peace movements in Japan. However, Hiroshima and Nagasaki continued to hold peace rallies on 6 and 9 August respectively, and the peace theme was re-echoed throughout the world, from New York's Union Square to Vienna, from France to Finland, West Germany to Tunisia. With the signing, in September 1951 at San Francisco, of the American-Japanese Peace Treaty, the way was clear for the Japanese to forge ahead with their movement to abolish nuclear weapons and establish world peace.

18

During those frustrating times of the American occupation Sumiteru and his survivor friends contented themselves with meeting informally, and thus fostered and maintained among themselves a spirit of mutual aid and solidarity. Several similar groups existed, few of them designated by name. One exception was the Young Women's Association of Nagasaki. Founded in 1953, it was not officially recognized. So far, no official body, least of all the Japanese Government, had done much to help the A-bomb survivors with their special problems.

It was at one of those meetings in Nagasaki that Sumiteru came to know Senzi Yamaguti, Yukie Tsuji and Tadashi Kokurawa. Senzi's plight was pitiful: he had passed through the technical college but nobody would give him a job because massive keloid formations disfigured him and prevented him from bending his right arm or turning his head. In 1952, when he was twenty-two, Senzi, in despair, tried to kill himself by cutting a vein in his arm; a friend found him just in time.

It was in April of that year, under the terms of the San Francisco treaty, that the American occupying forces left Japan. At last Japanese doctors, scientists and sociologists were able to go freely about their researches into the effects of the bombs of Hiroshima and Nagasaki. There were years of painstaking work ahead of them and their foreign, including US, collaborators. At the other end of the scale, among the A-bomb survivors, feeling against nuclear weapons was growing more and more intense and uniting them as a community with a common aim: a universal ban on nuclear weapons.

It was now more than six years since the bombing of

Hiroshima and Nagasaki. The restrictions imposed by the Americans during the occupation had kept the public in ignorance of details of the bomb's effects, particularly those on the human organism. Moreover, it was still too soon to assess many of the delayed effects.

Sumiteru and his survivor friends, when they met together, would discuss the information they had been able to pick up from the doctors and hospital staff during their regular visits for treatment – Sumiteru was still going for blood tests and the examination and dressing of the open wound on his back. By exchanging among themselves all this verbal information, and from the occasional medical reports now being published, the young A-bomb survivors were able to gain some idea of the bomb's cruel ravages on human flesh. If they were unable to grasp fully the technical details, they had no reason to doubt that the essential facts were true. The effects of the bomb on human beings were numerous, diverse and extremely disquieting.

They could be broadly divided into two stages: first, those that were immediate and acute and, secondly, the delayed effects. The main cause of death in the first stage was thermal injury, which Sumiteru, Senzi and Yukie, disfigured though they were, had managed to survive. They were the lucky ones; for thousands the damage to their skin was too extensive – either they were completely incinerated or so scorched and shrivelled that they succumbed within hours.

The survivors were left with ugly, permanent scars. One kind, hypertrophic scars, formed in the deeper tissue which would thicken and finally protrude from the skin surface. Others, keloids, consisted of tissue which overgrew the burnt flesh in irregular shapes resembling the shell and legs of a crab. It was mainly the young – primary school-children and teenagers, like Sumiteru and Senzi – who suffered from keloids, their young skin branded with grotesque, indelible marks. Keloids often restricted limb movement, as with Sumiteru's left arm and Senzi's neck; and being so unsightly they embarrassed and distressed the victim.

The effect of blast was mechanical; near the hypocentre it crushed people to death on the spot or tore out their heart, their lungs and their bowels. Within a thousand metres, the violent air pressure punctured ear-drums or injured eyeballs, and left the victim in a state of deep, perhaps incurable, shock.

The day after Hiroshima, President Truman had conceded publicly that it was an atomic bomb that had been dropped on the city. For the first time in history mankind had been exposed in mass to enormous doses of ionizing radiation: primary radiation, where the gamma rays and neutrons struck people directly, and secondary radiation, where the neutrons continued to emit radioactivity after being absorbed by various materials on the ground, the clothes and bodies of the dead and wounded or the dust and débris of the explosion which was carried sky-high in the mushroom-shaped atomic cloud to fall out later as 'ashes of death' or 'black rain' on unsuspecting people, on animals and vegetation some distance away.

With humans, the immediate symptoms of radioactive contamination included vomiting, bloody diarrhoea, bleeding gums, purpura (purplish blood patches beneath the skin), malaise, fever, loss of appetite and depilation (loss of hair). At the beginning, poisonous gas was suspected of having caused these symptoms, but Truman's talk of an atomic bomb confirmed to the Japanese that the symptoms were those of radioactive contamination – atomic sickness, they called it or, more precisely, radiation sickness. Many victims, Sumiteru, Yukie and Senzi among them, in time partly recovered. Thousands of others, closer to the burst-point or less shielded – like Tadashi's parents – were condemned, occasionally with a short respite, to death. None were entirely reprieved; they had to live out their days with some chronic complaint – with Tadashi himself it was stomach trouble – or in constant fear of cancer erupting in themselves or their offspring.

The deadly gamma and neutron rays penetrated deep into the body and if, in doing so, they lost some of their effect, they still damaged blood and tissue cells and blood-forming organs. The most radio-sensitive cells are found in the bone-marrow, but others are highly vulnerable: the lymphocytes and the cells of the intestine and stomach, of the respiratory system, urinary tract and the reproductive functions – testes and ovary. Once the blood was contaminated by radiation, red cells, white cells and platelets were diminished in number and in one or several of these organs there occurred internal haemorrhage, followed by infection which often proved fatal. Radiation also upset other body functions, causing anaemia, menstrual troubles in women and sterility in men. In the wake of these immediate effects of radiation many more were yet to manifest themselves as 'delayed effects'.

Radiation was the most important factor in carcinogenesis – the production of cancer – among those exposed to the atom bomb. The hardest hit were children between birth and ten years old. Cancer in different forms was found to be directly related to the atom bomb. Leukaemia, a wild increase of white blood cells, though its cause has not been discovered, is known to be provoked by radioactivity; confirmation comes from the sadly large number of radiologists – 'medical martyrs' – who have succumbed to the disease, among them the French woman Marie Curie, who invented that smooth-sounding but sinister expression 'radioactivity', and Dr Takashi Nagai, the oft-lamented poet of Nagasaki.

Among the 'early entrants' searching in the ruins for their loved ones, many fell victim to secondary radiation. Leukaemia among the 'early entrants' was three times higher than in the rest of Japan. Others who were caught in the snare were the volunteers, young and old, who hastened to help on the spot or in the temporary hospitals. Residual radioactivity in the victims' bodies and clothes killed or maimed not a few of those who came to their rescue. Among those exposed to the A-bomb, cases of leukaemia increased dramatically until 1952, after which the disease continued to make more ravages among the exposed than the unexposed.

The young were the most frequent victims of leukaemia, as they were of cancer of the thyroid, an endocrinic gland in the base of the neck. Though slow to declare itself, cancer of the thyroid became five times more frequent among the exposed than the unexposed. Again, more children and teenagers than adults figured on the death roll.

It was mostly the elderly who were struck down by lung cancer, caused partly by inhaling radioactive particles, partly by a high dose of radiation near the hypocentre. Lung cancer proved to be twice as powerful a killer among the exposed as among the rest of the population.

Breast cancer, it was found, was about four times higher than the national average among those exposed within one kilometre of the hypocentre. It was hardly surprising that young girls, their ages varying between ten and nineteen, were the most frequent victims.

It was the young, too, who were most vulnerable to cancer of the salivary glands, another small corner of the body affected by the A-bomb's lethal rays – and the younger the victims, the harder they were hit. With Truman's finger on the button and General Anami's contempt for his compatriots' lives, the atom bomb had functioned remarkably well as a means of destroying the young roots of the human race.

Still the atom bomb had not finished its aggression against human flesh. The eyes of those exposed were often grievously damaged, either directly by the searing heat or blast or by the delayed effects of radiation. The lens of the eye is sensitive to radioactivity. 'Atom bomb cataract' might occur several months or even years after exposure. That good man Ji-san was one of the victims. In consequence of his having wandered for three days among the radioactive ruins in search of Sumiteru, Ji-san developed a cataract in each eye which finally robbed him of his sight.

As with the young, the atom bomb's ionizing radiation was particularly cruel on women, were they virgins, mothers or mothers to be. It had the effect of delaying menarche, the beginning of menstruation. Amenorrhoea, the absence or delay of menstruation, happened frequently to women exposed to the bomb's radiation, which also tended to accelerate menopause by some two years.

A most vile and barbaric achievement of the A-bomb was to kill the young while they were still in their mother's womb. Young proliferating cells, such as those of the foetus, are extremely sensitive to low doses of radiation. Thus in the foetal stage, especially during the first fifteen weeks, the expected baby is at high risk from radiation which may fall on its mother. The younger the foetus and the higher the radiation dose received by the mother, the more immediate were the tragic consequences such as stillborn babies, or others who survived only a few months. Of those who did survive longer, many developed leukaemia, were mentally retarded, mongoloid or microcephalic (small-headed), or reduced in one way or another in stature – narrow shoulders and pelvis, funnel-chest. These are only a few from a long list of defects from which those unborn infants were condemned to suffer throughout their lives: myopia, strabismus, pharyngal troubles, teeth problems, hepatitis, cirrhosis, congenital cataract, obesity. There was reason, too, to suspect radiation of causing complicated changes in the body's cell structure: chromosomic aberrations and consequent genetic effects were discovered. More years of research were still needed to determine the truth. But it was already evident, if nuclear weapons left survivors, what pathetic sub-human creatures they would be.

While the American aim to end the war as soon as possible was laudable, was the atomic bomb justifiable or even necessary for the purpose? Or was its use a crime against humanity and indeed the human environment?

People, not excluding Japanese and Americans, were and always will be divided on the issue. Yet General Arnold, Chief of the US Army Air Forces, which were responsible for the mass air attacks, had previously assured Truman that 'conventional' bombing would be adequate to end the war without an American invasion of Japan. General Eisenhower, Commander-in-Chief of the Allied Forces which had recently defeated Germany, had told the President that the atomic bomb was not 'mandatory' in order to save American soldiers' lives. These seasoned military chiefs – two of the greatest – doubtless knew what they were talking about.

At that time the sole aim of air bombing was to destroy, materially and morally, an enemy already at war. In the case of the Japanese, a considerable weight of allied military, political and scientific opinion was against using the atomic bomb for that purpose. Its use as a deterrent, as a scarecrow to frighten a potential enemy from breaking the peace, was not yet in question.

Whether or not the atomic bombing of Hiroshima and Nagasaki constituted a crime, one thing is certain, as scientists and sociologists agree: the magnitude of destruction amounted, as no other single weapon has ever achieved, to genocide as well as sociocide, ecocide and biocide – in brief, the negation of life.

The anger of the Japanese public had first been vented, understandably, against the Americans. Then the opinion of the Japanese swung, just as logically, against their own government, or more precisely its military members. It was they, the argument now ran, who were primarily to blame, because they had led the nation into a war they could not win and, by insisting to the last on the country's going down in a suicidal defeat, had caused the wholesale murder of large numbers of its citizens. The 'one hundred million' were not so meek and stupid as their military leaders had believed, nor all that keen to 'die together', as the slogan went, to save the militarists' face.

The Japanese high command had been sheltering behind the dead of its civil population, waiting, hoping for the great military show-down on Japanese soil. On their side, the Americans had chosen to skip the military show-down and to fight, not against the Japanese armed forces who, strategically, were already beaten, but against defenceless civilians. In so doing, the Americans ran no danger of reprisals; US civilians were well out of range. The war had begun as a war between governments and their respective fighting forces. Both sides had allowed it to degenerate into a slaughter of Japanese civilians.

The rationale at first propagated by the Americans – that the Japanese civilian population had nobly sacrificed itself to rid the country of a military dictatorship, no longer cut any ice with the Japanese. They now realized that they had been massively victimized because their own leaders had refused to admit to evident defeat and because the Americans had decided to end the war, not by diplomacy (armed as it was), not by an invasion, costly in lives to both sides, but (as Hitler had once promised the British) by rasing enemy cities to the ground with bombs; bombs on Japanese cities would save American soldiers' lives. On military grounds the argument may have been sound, but from a moral standpoint, a civilized people like the Americans could hardly pretend that they were fighting a righteous war when it sought to obtain quick victory by the massive extermination of enemy non-combatants. Still less so when it used the atomic bomb which, no one could seriously deny, was an 'inhuman weapon'.

For the Americans it was obviously the easiest way out, for the Japanese the hardest, when unconditional surrender was the alternative. And so, Hiroshima and Nagasaki – and certainly worse, but for Russia's entry into the war against Japan.

19

In the six years since the end of the war the majority of A-bomb survivors who had not died or wasted away, had been drifting aimlessly and unwanted, uncertain of themselves and their future, searching for a convincing explanation for their broken lives. What had *they* done to deserve such terrible misfortune, was the question to which they sought an answer.

There were exceptions and Sumiteru was one. He had the advantage, it is true, of going back into a waiting job; but, seriously injured as he was, he managed to summon the will and the guts to surmount the constant depression and fatigue which weighed on him and to harness his enfeebled energies to his strenuous work. The knowledge of the A-bomb and its effects which he and his fellow-survivors had gained with the passing of the years had brought them closer together and formed solid ties among them. Their feelings and opinions had matured. They were beginning to discover a *raison d'être* – that there was, after all, a meaning in their lives, however shattered they had been; that their past, their present and – inescapably – their future sufferings were not for nothing. They were the survivors of the atom bomb, a unique community some 400,000 strong, the only people on earth who could speak at first hand about the consequences of an atom bomb attack, who could argue from experience the case – essentially human and moral as opposed to political – against the use of nuclear weapons. There began to spread among them a notion that they were a chosen people, a people with a mission, to oppose as long as they lived the rule of nuclear weapons, the rule of death for living creatures and replace it with the rule of life and respect for the fundamental truth that man is an individual who counts, and whose survival is dependent on his natural environment. Collectively they swore to devote their lives to obtaining a universal ban on nuclear weapons and, further, to the establishment of world peace. Thus they found a vocation, life-long and positive, to fill the emptiness, replace the despair of the past. As yet they were not nationally organized. Their movement had yet to be publicly accepted; for that it needed something to give it impetus.

It came, in the form of a gigantic, blinding explosion, on 1 March 1954. That day, at Bikini, a coral atoll in the Marshall Islands, America's thermo-nuclear hydrogen bomb, 'Bravo', pulverized the little island into millions of tons of radioactive dust. The hydrogen bomb had grown out of the panic caused by the explosion, in August 1949, of Russia's first atom bomb – the bomb of which Truman had said: 'They will never make one.' The following year, 1950, Truman gave the go-ahead for the horrific weapon which was to be the hydrogen bomb. Characteristically, he ignored the advice of his senior advisers, notably David Lilienthal, chairman of the US Atomic Energy Commission and the AEC's advisory board. 'We must keep ahead,' he kept on telling them – in the arms race which the President had himself started.

Later he began to get cold feet. 'This isn't a military weapon,' he remarked, 'it is used to wipe out women and children and unarmed people,' as if his Hiroshima and Nagasaki bombs had not already done the same thing. Yet Truman had come a little way since then. Though he had once vaunted himself as the man who had pulled the trigger of the Hiroshima bomb, not to mention the Nagasaki one, the President was beginning to have second thoughts about future bombs.

America's thermo-nuclear hydrogen bomb, when the details became known, shocked the world. A fifteen-megaton bomb, it was equivalent to well over one thousand Hiroshima uranium bombs, or nearly seven hundred Nagasaki plutonium ones. The hydrogen bomb, the product of nuclear fission, signified for the first time man's capacity to destroy all life on earth, if not the planet itself.

When Sumiteru heard the news of Bikini his first thought was for the fall-out. Who is going to get it? he wondered. The answer was not long in coming. The Americans had obligingly, but with complete disregard for the Bikinians' love of their land and culture, evacuated them to other islands in the Micronesian group, considered a safe distance from the explosion. The formidable cloud of radioactive coral particles was carried aloft, where it met high altitude winds which had unexpectedly shifted in direction. They swept the atomic cloud over three inhabited islands upon which the radioactive particles began to fall. Two hundred and thirty-nine Marshall-islanders were contaminated; forty-six of them later died. Twenty-eight US observers on Longelap Island were also caught by the fall-out, as was the twenty-three-man crew of the Japanese tuna-fishing vessel *Fukuryu Maru* No 5, 'Lucky Dragon No 5', which was sailing just outside the prescribed danger zone. With all but one or two of its crew showing the usual symptoms of radiation sickness, the vessel made back at full speed to its base at Yaizu, in Shizuoka prefecture, one hundred kilometres or so down the coast from Tokyo. There, tons of contaminated fish were immediately destroyed; the crew were rushed to hospital where one of them later died from the delayed effects of radiation. His grieving widow and family received from the US Government the meagre pittance of one million yen, that is US$3,800.

The *Fukuryu Maru* incident raised an outcry throughout Japan against nuclear weapons. The scattered groups of atom bomb survivors got together and identified themselves with the victims of the *Fukuryu Maru* and the Marshall islanders in the name of the '*Hibakusha*'* – H-bomb and A-bomb victims. They demanded the abolition of nuclear weapons – complete and absolute abolition with no bargains made on the side by this or that nuclear power. At that date there were but three, the USA, the USSR and the UK.

The Japanese protest was immediately taken up by other

* pronounced *Hibak'sha*

countries. In the US, the *Scientific American* argued that the thermo-nuclear bomb had become too big to be entrusted to the rulers in Washington. *Newsweek* warned Americans that, if they lived in a strategically important city, the odds against survival in an H-bomb war were a million to one. In London a group of housewives banded together to protest publicly against further nuclear tests. Their small committee became known in time as the Campaign for Nuclear Disarmament. Before the year was out Bertrand Russell, the celebrated British philosopher, mathematician and Nobel Prize winner, produced a manifesto which raised the question: Shall we put an end to the human race or shall mankind renounce war? Among the several Nobel Prize winners who signed the manifesto was Albert Einstein. The aged genius had never ceased to feel remorse for the letter he had written in 1939 to Roosevelt, urging the US President to procure stocks of uranium; it had led to the Manhattan project. Einstein signed the manifesto in April 1955. Two days later he died.

In Japan, all through 1955, feelings on the nuclear issue ran high and new anti-nuclear groups were forming, especially in the Hiroshima and Nagasaki prefectures. On 6 August – that mournful anniversary – hundreds of Japanese, joined by delegates from a dozen foreign countries, flocked to Hiroshima for the first World Conference against H- and A-bombs. Two months later the young male survivors of Nagasaki, caught up in the enthusiasm for anti-nuclear protest groups, decided it was time to found one of their own. Sumiteru was one of the thirty founder members; so were Senzi Yamaguti and Tadashi, now nineteen. Early the following year the young men's group joined up with the Young Women's Association which had been going for three years. They now called themselves the Young Men's and Young Women's *Hibakusha* Association of Nagasaki. Their sworn and unalterable aim was a universal ban – nothing less – on nuclear weapons, and the establishment of world peace.

The sworn aim of the *Hibakusha*, idealist and ambitious as it looked, was deeply sincere, inspired as it was by the simple fact that they alone could speak at first hand of the A-bomb's immediate and permanent effects on the human body, on the human mind. Sumiteru's devotion to the cause was personal, passionate and complete. He now saw a meaning in all his years of suffering and felt no more regrets. He could say to himself: 'Thank God I fought and won my fight for survival.' He felt convinced that he had survived for a definite – and predestined – purpose: to help without relenting in the fight against nuclear warfare, and if it came to that, against all warfare. He was determined, as long as he remained alive, not to spare himself.

20

There was one thing that worried Sumiteru: he was still shy of
the unsightly scars which disfigured nearly half his body. It was
in August 1955, after the Hiroshima conference, when the
young *hibakusha* were filled with elation and passion for their
cause, that Sumiteru at last freed himself of his complex.
August was a sad month for the *hibakusha*; no doubt the
stifling, humid heat was one reason, but there was something
else too. Memories of those dreadful days of August 1945
would float up to the surface of the *hibakushas'* minds, bringing
with them a malaise and heaviness of heart mingled with that
sinister ambiance of death and desolation. There is not a
hibakusha who does not feel this strange August-psychosis,
though so many years have passed.

If Sumiteru's scarred back always bothered him, it was
during those sweltering August days that he felt it most. The
flash-burn which had struck him was of such intensity that it
destroyed the sweat glands over its entire surface as well as
damaging the tissue cells. In the heat of summer his back was
so uncomfortably hot that it felt as if it were covered by a layer
of cotton wool; in winter, on the other hand, it felt so icy cold
that it kept him awake at night.

To break the depressing spell of August, Sumiteru and a
dozen *hibakusha* friends, boys and girls, decided to go swimming at one of the local beaches. The anti-H and A-bomb
conference in Hiroshima and the annual peace memorial
service at Nagasaki, with all the intense emotions those two
events engendered, were now over. A few days later those
young *hibakushas* decided to have some fun. They took the

blue and silver bus to Tobo-no-hama, a forty-minute ride eastward through the hills.

Tobo-no-hama means the place from where you can see the east. The bay is surrounded by mountains which, like those of Mourne in Ireland, sweep down to the sea. The sea faithfully reflects the sky – blue in fair weather, grey when it is dull. Today, sky and sea merged in a boundless expanse of matching blue. The ebb-tide had left uncovered the beach of fine grey sand crowded with holiday-makers; Tobo-no-hama was one of the most popular beaches within reach of Nagasaki.

The place was known, too, because of its covered vegetable market. During the war people would go out there from Nagasaki by any means available – in the rare bus, by bicycle or even on foot – to buy fruit and vegetables direct from the neighbouring farmers whose produce, for want of transport, did not reach the markets of Nagasaki. Tobo-no-hama had a reputation for its climate – the sea breezes and the pine-scented wind off the mountains were known for their curative properties. There existed a sanatorium for chest diseases at Tobo-no-hama.

But it was not for their health that Sumiteru and his friends were there that day. After the solemn anniversary service at Nagasaki today was the day to wipe away tears, to celebrate their survival from that catastrophe. Tobo-no-hama was the place. They stripped off their clothes and changed into swimming suits – all except Sumiteru. He always explained to his friends that he kept on his shirt to protect his back from the sun. That was less than the whole truth. Sumiteru could not find the courage to expose the shocking scar on his back to the public gaze.

All the same, he raced on the sand with his friends, laughed and swam with them. Then one of them shouted: 'Come on Sumi-san, off with your shirt! Let's show everybody that we are the *hibakusha* who survived the A-bomb and never want to see another!' They crowded round Sumiteru, snatching at his shirt, but he was quicker than they. Some kind of frenzy seized him, and it was he who made the decisive gesture. He dragged his shirt over his head, off his body, and with a triumphant cry threw it into the air. Carried away by the excitement of the others he shouted for the benefit of everyone within earshot: 'There I am, scarred all over. It was the atom bomb which did this to me when I was sixteen. Don't turn your eyes away from me, but look at what the bomb did to me and thousands of others. Join me and my *hibakusha* friends, please join us in saying: "No more atom bombs, never! Nagasaki must be the last!"'

While his friends cheered, the people around him on the beach clapped approvingly. It was not like Sumiteru to indulge in such extravagant caperings, but the excitement of his friends had been too much for him. He ran towards the sea and plunged into the waves. He had, at least momentarily, rid himself both of his shirt and the shaming stigma of his hideous scars.

Sumiteru was swimming alone now, slowly, and thinking lucidly: I am strong again; I must no longer be ashamed of my scars; they are honourable scars of battle. They must be the proof of my sincerity in the fight against nuclear weapons. He was convinced by his own logic. Yet his mind was still troubled by those indelible scars. His circle of friends, within the *hibakusha* and beyond it, included many girls. Sumiteru got on well with most of them. When a schoolboy he had played tricks on the girl pupils, but they liked him all the same because he was never unkind or mean to them. Being so small and mischievous, they liked him and took him for the mascot of his class. Now, he reflected sadly, most of those boys and girls were dead – killed by the bomb. He was no longer anyone's mascot. But in the years between Sumiteru had matured. Girls enjoyed his company; they were charmed by his manner and his good looks – so long as he was fully clothed. They saw him as a most pleasing companion, but not as a partner in marriage – for there was not one among them who had not heard of his terrible disfigurement. He talked to his most faithful friend, his grandfather Ji-san, about his desire to marry, and Ji-san in time produced a list of eligible maidens.

It was a regular system in Japan, marriage by arrangement. Sumiteru discussed marriage with these girls, one after the other, but not one of them would accept him. The way some of them refused him distressed him deeply. To his proposal they would reply unkindly: 'Why should I marry you, when you are all covered in scars?' Others were sweet and understanding, but no less firm in their refusal. Among them was a girl who was not on Ji-san's list. Sumiteru would never mention her name. He loved her, and she him. He would take her to the theatre or the movies, or to dine in one or other of those simply furnished, cosy little restaurants to be found in the narrow streets of Nagasaki. In winter, late in the evening, they would stroll round the floodlit port, and when, in summer, the days lengthened, they would walk up on the hill, talking of themselves and of the problems of a future together. Yet the day came when she told him gently: 'I'm sorry, Sumi-san, I cannot marry you.'

Her words did not come as a surprise to Sumiteru. He was expecting them and was even a little surprised that they had not come sooner. But they saddened him. It seemed that all of him beneath the surface – his sincerity, his fortitude – pleased women. They were the essence of him. But those foul scars branded all over his body were his undoing. They threatened his life – life as he longed for it to be, as a husband and a father. Sumiteru felt very depressed.

Luckily for him he had many good friends. They helped to cheer him through his long and wearying hours of work. It was when he returned home and they were no longer there, that his mood changed and black clouds of despair descended upon him. It did not take Oba-chan long to notice. Now in very poor health and bed-ridden, the old lady was all the more upset by her grandson's melancholic expression.

21

Sumiteru had an aunt, Osa Taguchi, who, like Oba-chan, adored him. She came regularly to the house to look after Oba-chan. Osa, of course, shared Oba-chan's concern for Sumiteru; the boy was obviously unhappy. Having had no luck with Ji-san's list of 'possibilities', Sumiteru confided to his aunt his longing to marry and his doubts at ever being able to find a girl willing to accept him. Osa, of course, passed everything on to Oba-chan and the two old ladies began to plan for Sumiteru's future happiness.

Aunt Osa had a friend living in Togitsu, who, as it happened, was none other than Eiko's mother. Osa had once met the girl in her home – a good, sensible girl with pleasing looks, she told Oba-chan – but at the request of Eiko's mother, she had already proposed her to another man. It had happened before Sumiteru had mentioned his own problem to Osa. In any case, Eiko had made it clear that she was in no mind to marry anyone. However, Oba-chan, ever ready to defend her grandson, exclaimed a little irritably: 'But Osa-san, what do you think you're doing? This girl Eiko is the girl for Sumiteru!' Slightly abashed at not having already raised the point, Aunt Osa agreed to approach Eiko and her mother.

Next day she took the train from Nagasaki to Michinoo, then, despite the blustery February day, she made the forty-five-minute walk to Noda. Eiko's mother was at home. So, too, was Eiko; she had come in from the fields for lunch, the usual boiled rice, vegetables and fish which her mother would always buy from the fishermen on the quayside at Togitsu. Aunt Osa asked Eiko: 'Have you thought any more about marriage?'

'No,' replied Eiko bluntly. 'I'm so busy all day I haven't time to think of marrying.'

Eiko was now twenty-five. She had been at work, hard, unsparing, lonely work in all weathers, for some ten years. After recovering from malaria, she had spent two years at the Togitsu Youth School and, true to form, had gained mentions for both her studies and her conduct. Class-work, she had found, was sheer relief after toiling in the fields, a job which somehow she found the strength to combine with her studies, as Sumiteru's sister Keiko had once done on Oba-chan's small-holding. Her schooling over for good, it was the land which henceforth, without respite, occupied her day.

It was not a job for the sophisticated, working in the paddy, knee-deep in water, planting rice seedlings. She wore a loose blouse and *mompei*, baggy trousers rolled up to her knees, long socks and straw sandals to protect her legs and feet from leeches. Work in the dry fields demanded *jikatavi*, the curious Japanese flexible boot which leaves the big toe protruding and all the others covered. This loose-fitting dress, resistant both to heat and cold, was topped by the customary head-cloth and, in summer, a shady straw hat. Stooping for hours in the paddy, or hoeing the dry ground did not worry Eiko. She was happy; the fields of Noda were so calm, with just the song and the flight of birds, the whispering wind and the distant voices of other men and girls working, like her, their own particular plot. Often, when her own work was finished, Eiko would go and help them and thus earn a few extra *yen*. Sometimes she went with them in the evening to the movies. She enjoyed her life and her work. The result of her labours, the first tender green shoots of the rice seedlings and vegetables, the budding of the fruit trees, brought her ample, if simple, reward.

As Aunt Osa talked to Eiko and her mother she was struck by the goodness of this girl, by her simple, straightforward manner, her generous character. To Eiko's mother Osa said: 'I would like to propose to Eiko a young man of twenty-six, that is a year older than her. His name is Sumiteru Taniguchi. He is a good boy, rather quiet in manner and a very courageous worker, despite his wounds. He was burned by the atom bomb, but the scars on his face have disappeared thanks to plastic surgery, and those on his arms and legs have healed well enough so as not to be noticeable.' Aunt Osa did not mention Sumiteru's back.

Without having given much thought to what Osa had been saying, Eiko thanked her, bowing, and went on hurriedly: 'Forgive me, I must leave you. I have some things to finish in the fields, then I have to get into Nagasaki by six o'clock.' It was still early in the year and the land did not demand a full day of Eiko's time; she had taken a temporary evening job in a small Nagasaki restaurant, travelling from her home and back by bus.

When Aunt Osa returned to Oba-chan's house in the evening, Sumiteru was just back from work. As usual, he looked tired and depressed. He and Osa bowed and greeted each other. 'Cheer up, Sumi-san,' she said to him. 'I have found a nice girl for you and we are going to see her tomorrow.' Sumiteru thanked her without much enthusiasm. How could this girl ever replace the one he had lost?

At Oba-chan's bedside all three discussed the prospect. 'She spent most of her childhood in Korea,' said Osa and began to sketch Eiko's *curriculum vitae*. 'Though she never felt the war as we all did, she always had good mentions for her civic duties and her studies, too. I'm convinced that she's a generous and good-natured girl who is not afraid of hard work. She has a look about her that I like – not very tall, but composed and pretty-looking. Her father was doing well for himself as a builder in Seoul and started up again as soon as he got back to Japan after the war. Eiko lost two brothers killed in action, so the family is honourable and respected. She has an elder brother and a twin sister. Seriously, Sumi-san,' Aunt Osa concluded, 'I think Eiko is a girl who will stick to you and look after you – and that is what you need above all.'

Sumiteru had been listening without saying a word; now he just muttered: 'Thank you, Aunt Osa.' Oba-chan had clung to Osa's every word.

'Listen, dear Sumi-san,' she said, 'we have known each other all your life. If I have been hard with you sometimes, you know you deserved it. You know too that always I have wanted the best for you.'

'Yes, Oba-chan,' Sumiteru cut in, 'you have been good to me all my life, like Ji-san. You know how much I am indebted to you.'

Oba-chan went on: 'Sumi-san, listen to me; you have seen me bed-ridden nearly a year. You have been good to me, too. I want to tell you – my end is not far off, I know it. I shall be happy to go if only, before I do so, I see you married to someone who will take care of you as I have always done.'

Sumiteru bowed to his grandmother. '*Arigato gozayimasu* – thank you very much, Oba-chan. I trust for your sake and mine, that all will turn out as you wish.'

'I'm sure it will,' put in Aunt Osa. 'I will meet you tomorrow after work at the post office, Sumiteru, and take you to the restaurant where Eiko works. It's quite close, in Edo-machi.'

For all the solicitude and the kind intentions of his grandmother and aunt, Sumiteru was not in the best of tempers as he went to work, down the hill and across the ferry next morning. How could they imagine that this unknown girl Eiko could ever replace the girl he had loved – and lost? The day dragged on and at 5.30 p.m. Sumiteru ranged his red bicycle as usual at the main post office and clocked off.

Aunt Osa was waiting for him. 'Come on, Sumi-san, don't look so down-hearted. We will walk the few hundred metres to the restaurant.' Ten minutes later they stood in front of the door which Sumiteru pushed open for his aunt; he followed her inside. It was a small restaurant with a row of rectangular tables down one side, a bar on the other and, beyond, an open kitchen. They sat side by side at a table from which they could command a discreet view of the kitchen. At that moment Eiko was making a *kaiten yaki*, a kind of cake. Lowering her voice Aunt Osa said: 'Look, Sumi-san, that girl in the kitchen – that is Eiko.'

Eiko had no idea of their presence in the restaurant and,

while she went about her job, Sumiteru had time to observe her. Still in his awkward mood, he said to Osa: 'Well, she may well be a nice girl, but I don't see anything special about her.' Eiko put her *Kaiten Yaki* in the oven and, a moment later, came out of the kitchen. Aunt Osa beckoned to her. She came over to the table, and bowed to Osa and Sumiteru, who did likewise. 'Hullo, Eiko,' Osa began. 'You remember me? I have brought Taniguchi-san to talk to you. Sit down with us.'

Eiko sat opposite them. Osa went on: 'Taniguchi-san is looking for a wife and I believe you are the girl for him.' Sumiteru then spoke a few grudging words to Eiko, asking her about herself and her work and telling her a little about himself. But, thought Eiko, this young man speaks in such an off-hand way, how can I ever get on with him?

Aloud she said: 'No, I am not at present in any mind to marry.' And so the subject was not pursued; yet as Eiko served them she and Sumiteru were taking each other in. At the end of the meal she brought the *kaiten yaki* she had been making. It was good and Sumiteru thought: Well, at least she knows how to cook.

As Osa and Sumiteru left the restaurant Osa said to Eiko: 'Eiko dear, Taniguchi-san's offer of marriage still stands. Think it over and let me know.'

For some days Eiko pondered. Taniguchi-san was obviously a nice young man, but he had such an arrogant manner. He was good-looking, but then there were those scars on his arms and legs that Osa had spoken about. Five days later she sent a message to Osa, thanking her but saying quite simply she declined Sumiteru's offer of marriage.

Sumiteru had not been much more enthusiastic at first. But though he remained sulky and reluctant, his aunt did not cease to persuade him. 'Come on, Sumi-san, you have been turned down by every girl to whom you have proposed. Eiko has turned you down too, but I am certain that with a little more persuasion she will accept you. Come on, Sumi-san!' She encouraged him: 'You have been so unhappy and, another thing, so has Oba-chan on your account, and Ji-san too. She is near the end of her days. Make her happy before she dies – make your mind up to marry Eiko and leave the rest to me.'

Sumiteru thought about Osa's words. Though it was certainly not his last chance of marriage, he had to admit that so far, every girl had turned him down. If Eiko would accept him, well, that would solve matters. He told Osa, who went once again to see Eiko in her home. 'Taniguchi-san so badly wants you to accept him,' she told her. 'Besides, Eiko, you are twenty-five and it will get more and more difficult for you to find such a nice man.' Eiko felt incapable of resisting the persuasive Osa. It was not that she really wanted marriage with Sumiteru – she just felt resigned to it.

'All right, I agree to marry Sumiteru-san,' she said, calling him by his forename for the first time.

Eiko and Sumiteru were married ten days later, on 10 March, in Oba-chan's home, where Eiko met her future husband's family for the first time. She was accompanied by her parents, her brother, her sister and Yoshie, her sister-in-law. Sumiteru's bad mood had passed, but she was still hoping that he would not be quite so authoritative all his life. He led her by the hand to Oba-chan's bedside and presented her to the old lady. Eiko bowed low; Oba-chan held out a feeble hand. 'Give me your hand, child,' she said kindly to Eiko, who obeyed. She could feel sympathy in the old lady's touch. 'Listen. My Sumi-san has lived with me all his life. He is a good boy, but he needs a lot of care. I know you are a good and a brave girl and will take care of him. Thank you, Eiko-san. I wish you both every happiness.'

Ji-san was obviously pleased at his first sight of Eiko. 'Take good care of the boy,' he told her. Teiji and Keiko, Sumiteru's brother and sister who had come over with their father Sadamachi from Osaka, after exchanging their ritual bows, chatted with Eiko in so friendly a way that she felt her shyness changing into a liking for this family. But she noticed that all of them introduced at one time or another during the conversation one recurring, insistent phrase, spoken not imperatively

143

but more as a prayer: 'Take care of Sumiteru, he needs a lot of care.'

The morning ceremony was an entirely private affair during which liberal quantities of *sake* assured a warm atmosphere between the two families. Then the couple, with their closest relations, including Aunt Osa, drove down to the city hall, where their marriage was registered. Afterwards, warmer still from more *sake* and the happiness of the occasion, they repaired to Oba-chan's home on the hill. The celebrating this time was among friends, mostly Sumiteru's. It was something of an ordeal for Eiko, for she was meeting them for the first time. Again, she noticed this phrase was always on their lips: 'Take care of Sumiteru.' It seemed that Sumiteru's family and friends were all counting on her and leaving her a great responsibility.

It was true. Eiko realized, that she alone would in future have to be responsible for the care hitherto provided for Sumiteru by his family and friends. As they all crowded about him, downing *sake* after *sake* to his health, Eiko felt a bit left out. But already she began to feel the challenge – she would show them how devoted she could be to their friend, her husband. Poor Eiko, her loyalty was yet to be put to the test.

The party ended, the guests departed. It was late in the evening. A room had been arranged for the bridal couple; two beds were made up side by side on the floor. As the celebrations progressed, a mounting feeling of anxiety, which he was careful to hide, had taken hold of Sumiteru. He felt convinced that Aunt Osa had mentioned nothing to Eiko about his hideously scarred back. Otherwise his young bride would never have been so relaxed. Towards the end of the afternoon he had put a call through to the Midoriya Inn at Unzen, high up in the mountains, where he had often been with his bachelor friends. He reserved a room for two, with a bath.

Sumiteru reckoned that he could not possibly reveal his back to Eiko on this first evening of his marriage and under Oba-chan's roof. He and Eiko took to their separate beds; they were not, after all, in love. But in the dark Sumiteru whispered to Eiko: 'Tomorrow we will go to Unzen for a short honeymoon.' Come what might, he wanted Eiko to know the truth.

22

Next morning, after bidding *sayonara* to Oba-chan, Ji-san and Aunt Osa – who, all of them being in the know, were praying for the best – Sumiteru and Eiko walked down to the bus terminal opposite the station, each carrying a *furoshiki* in which they had wrapped a few things. There, to see them off, was one of Sumiteru's best friends, Susuma Nagata. As the bus made ready to leave Susuma came to the window where Eiko was seated and, looking her straight in her brown eyes, said with a hint of urgency: 'Please take great care of Sumiteru.' Then the bus was gone.

After threading its way through Nagasaki's busy morning traffic it was soon climbing steeply eastwards out of the valley. The lower slopes of the thickly wooded hills had been cleared and were cut into terraces where rice would soon be planted. Further on, the bus pierced clean through the hillside in a dark, dripping tunnel and on emerging swung north to Isahaya.

Eiko and Sumiteru had not said much to each other, but on passing through Isahaya he began to hark back, without too much detail, to those dark days in August 1945 – how he had been brought half-dead to Isahaya by his grandfather Ji-san, how he finally found his way back to Nagasaki via Nogaya. He purposely kept off the subject of his back; the bus was not the place to explain or apologize or beg for understanding. No, Sumiteru would wait till they were settled in at the Midoriya Inn and there, with as few words as possible, he would tell his wife about the problem which weighed so heavily on him.

There were enough things to talk about and see through the window to enable the young couple to keep up an effortless, if sporadic, conversation. Eiko told Sumiteru about Korea and how, when the Emperor announced the war's end, everyone wept; she remarked how terrible it must have been for Sumiteru, lying there so badly hurt in Isahaya. She had noticed that now, once the marriage ceremonies were over, Sumiteru's attitude had softened noticeably. He spoke gently and was attentive to her needs. She in turn felt kindly towards him and closer to him. The thought came to her: This must be the real Sumiteru. It's true what everybody was saying: 'He needs taking care of.'

The bus rolled on comfortably across wide stretches of rice-land, up over a low range of hills, then down towards the sea. It passed through two or three small fishing villages, with their nets and lobsterpots put out to dry, their Buddhist and Shinto temples and an occasional Christian church. A big tanker lay out in the bay. There was no lack of sights to keep the conversation going. Then the bus turned away from the seaside and began its abrupt climb to Unzen, where the mountain slopes were densely, luxuriantly wooded with tall, slim fire trees – millions of them – upon which the sun fell, glistening, and piercing the shade beneath with bright, straight shafts. A few moments later the bus was running into Unzen. Sumiteru and Eiko got down at the terminal and, carrying their light baggage, began walking briskly up the main street towards the Midoriya Inn. The mountain air was clear, but crisp and cold after the sheltered waterside of Nagasaki.

There was no more perfect place that Sumiteru could have chosen for the shocking revelation, followed, he hoped, by the delicate rapprochement which he had yet to make with his bride. The little holiday resort of Unzen might have been any small town in Europe – from Scotland to Sussex, from Austria to the Alpes Maritimes. Japan, after all, lies beyond the Far East; in climate and vegetation and to some extent mentality it is the link between East and West. Sumiteru knew the hotel of old. He had spent many a weekend there. Dating from 1875, during the Meiji period, it was well known and, to the satisfaction of Mr Fukuda, its proprietor, well frequented by a clientèle which came from as near as Nagasaki and as far away as Bangkok, Hong-Kong and Shanghai, and included Germans, French and Englishmen.

In appearance and character it was entirely Japanese – Japanese food, drink and hospitality, Japanese furniture and decoration. The Midoriya was a rectangular building which, with its two storeys, its double-tiered roof, the top covered with red, the lower with black tiles, its wooden beams and uprights and white stucco walls, was inviting enough to the visitor. Its intrinsic charm was considerably increased by its situation. It backed onto a steep, pine-covered hill; in front a wide space was planted with pine trees, some tall and growing free, others pruned into tight, round bundles. Across this open, tree-clad space there rushed a mountain stream.

It was in this homely little paradise that Sumiteru intended to reveal to Eiko his tragic problem. For him it was to be the moment of truth. Eiko suspected nothing. In the last twenty-four hours, left to themselves, she and Sumiteru had certainly become more friendly, if not yet intimate. She was neither unhappy nor afraid; she had not forgotten her mother's last words: 'Good luck, Eiko; but if it doesn't work out, you just come straight back to me!' As far as Eiko could tell it looked as if things would work out.

They spent the afternoon inside, the weather was so cold. Then Sumiteru said: 'Eiko, let's dine first, then take a bath and go to bed.' Eiko agreed. The three-hour bus-ride and the cold weather had given her an appetite. She enjoyed her dinner and drank a fresh fruit squash. Sumiteru was hungry too and he drank well, but not excessively – he felt he had to keep his wits about him and limited himself to a few glasses of his favourite beer, Kirin, knowing no more than the majority of Japanese that this famous Japanese beer was originally promoted by that canny, popular Scot who had come to Nagasaki a hundred years earlier – Thomas Blake Glover.

Over the meal they talked quietly of this and that, though Sumiteru's thoughts were racing continually some way ahead, to the time they would return to their bedroom. His feelings had settled down in these last twenty-four hours. He was resolved to go through with undressing, to expose his hideous disfigurement, and did not foresee any embarrassment as far as he was concerned. But if Eiko, when she saw his back, was shocked to the point of wanting to break up the marriage, he would regret it. He had taken a liking to Eiko; he wanted her to stay with him.

They walked to their room, and at their leisure began to undress. After a few moments they each stood in a kimono. 'Come on, Eiko,' Sumiteru invited her. 'Let's go into the bathroom.' The room was full of steam. The bath, a square wooden tub sunk into the floor, had already been run and was full of hot water; next to it a small compartment contained a can of scalding hot water for topping up the bath. Beside it stood two small stools and a couple of handbasins. Sumiteru faced Eiko as they sat, each on their stool, scooping water out of the bath and dousing themselves – a Japanese never washes in a bath, and before stepping into it he rinses off the soap.

The moment had come. 'Eiko, please wash my back,' asked Sumiteru and he half turned his back towards her, watching her all the time. He saw Eiko's face fall; from it faded all warmth and expression; she said nothing, but seemed to be momentarily paralysed. Then Sumiteru saw that her eyes were filled with tears which started rolling down her cheeks. He took her hand. 'It was the atom bomb,' he said sympathetically. 'I will tell you more about it later. Eiko, believe me, I never meant to deceive you, only finding that you had never been warned, I wanted you to see and to know everything.'

Eiko controlled her crying. Her reactions had followed each other in swift succession. The first was one of physical shock and revulsion. Next she felt hurt: I have been tricked into marriage with this poor wreck of a man. But then Eiko was filled with compassion; she immediately dismissed the thought for another. He is kind and good. He is my husband and he needs me. Everyone has told me that I am the only one who can save him. I shall stick to him. 'Come on, Sumiteru,' she said, 'let me wash your back.'

There were two beds laid out on the floor. Eiko and Sumiteru slept together in one of them.

Next day, Eiko was unusually quiet. Outwardly she appeared calm, but in her mind she was trying to rationalize the situation. Last night Sumiteru had consoled her with real affection and sympathy, but here was a new day; there would be hundreds and thousands more days during which she would have to live with Sumiteru and his poor, shattered body. Doubt crept into her mind; would she be able to bear it? She recalled the words of her mother: 'Come back home if things don't work out.' The thought tempted Eiko, challenging her declared loyalty to her husband.

It was so cold that they did not go out – a pity, thought Sumiteru, who saw that Eiko's mind was troubled and who feared a change of heart on her part. A stroll through the little town or in the countryside would have helped to distract her; instead, he had to make do with his own conversation. He told her about his boyhood on the hill and his job as a postman during the war; but he took care to end his tale before the atom bomb and the hellish years that followed.

Eiko listened absently, and Sumiteru felt the atmosphere was unbearably strained. But after a time she began to respond, until, with enjoyment it seemed to Sumiteru, she started telling him about her girlhood in Korea and her years working on the family holding at Noda. At last they met on common ground – the hill above Nagasaki and the fields at Noda; her job on the land, his on his red bicycle delivering mail. Eiko looked at Sumiteru and smiled: 'Well,' she said, 'at least we both know what it is to do a tough, all-weather job.' She felt more sure of herself; she knew her mind now and would never change it. She would stick to him; he needed her.

Next day, hand in hand, they walked to the bus terminal, stopping on the way to buy a few trinkets – souvenirs which would always remind them of those two critical days in Unzen. They held hands all through the three-hour ride back to Nagasaki. Now there was no need to keep the conversation going. They spoke only when they had something to say, not to break the silence as on the outward journey. They were getting to know each other.

Since their departure three days ago, Oba-chan, Ji-san and Aunt Osa had been wondering anxiously, would Sumi-san bring his bride back with him? Or would he return down-hearted, as they had so often seen him in the past, to announce: 'I've been rejected because of my scars.' Towards the middle of the third afternoon a knock came at Oba-chan's door. 'It's us,' cried two voices in unison, and in a moment Sumiteru and Eiko had slipped off their shoes and crossed the threshold of Oba-chan's home. Holding hands they made straight for the room of the old lady, by whose bedside Ji-san and Aunt Osa were quietly chatting. As Eiko and Sumiteru entered they all started up. 'Why, you all look so surprised,' Eiko exclaimed smiling. 'Well, let me say, no one is more surprised than Sumi-san and I. We are looking forward to a happy life together.'

Oba-chan, raising her hand feebly towards Eiko, said: 'Come here, my child, and let me take your hand. You are a good and a brave girl. I knew it from the beginning. I knew you had the courage to stay with Sumi-san. You have made me happy.'

Oba-chan was now very feeble and nearing the end. During her last few days, Eiko was continually at her bedside, comforting her, talking of Sumi-san and reassuring her that, like Sumiteru's sister Keiko, she would continue the family line, she hoped with a boy.

One evening, ten days after their return to Oba-chan's home, Eiko and Sumiteru heard Ji-san calling. 'Come quickly,' he said. 'She is very near the end.'

They both hurried to the bedside of Oba-chan, who recognized them. They heard her whisper: 'Farewell, my little Sumi-san; farewell my brave Eiko — always take care of him as I have done.' She tried to raise her hand, but it fell back limply on the bed. Oba-chan's heart had stopped beating.

Two days later Oba-chan's shrunken little body, on a simple wheeled bier, was taken by Ji-san and his grandchildren down to the municipal crematorium, just below where that teeming slum, the Ants' City, used to be. It was an impassive cuboid building, a shade sinister, through whose dark-tinted windows could just be discerned the mortuary chamber, the place of final parting before the dead, rich and poor, wise and foolish, good and evil, were reduced by fire into one common, indistinguishable form – ashes. Behind the crematorium, the stacks of empty bottles – beer, coke and seven-up – bore witness to the fact that the thirst for life of those left behind had not been impaired.

The following day Sumiteru and Eiko accompanied Ji-san, carrying the urn containing the ashes, to Nagayo. There, in the Buddhist temple, Oba-chan's ashes were buried among those of her ancestors.

With Ji-san, Sumiteru and Eiko returned to the house on the hill above Nagasaki. For some time, it was to be their own home, shared with Ji-san and his son Mitzuyoshi, his wife and their little girl.

23

Eiko and Sumiteru decided from the start that this mixture of households under one roof was going to work. They were thankful enough to have any roof – for Sumiteru it was a beloved old one – over their heads. Sumiteru had a lasting affection for Ji-san, and Eiko was already beginning to love the brave and generous old man whose hair was now thinning and whose sight, thanks to atom-bomb cataracts, was failing. As for Mitzuyoshi – well, he was certainly a good dozen years older than Sumiteru, but there was no reason why that should create problems between the two couples. Eiko and Sumiteru decided to keep quietly to their corner of the house and make do. Sumiteru was working an eight-hour shift at the post office – sometimes the morning shift, at other times the afternoon or the midnight one. He and Eiko found this variety convenient – it saved them from falling in too closely with the more monotonous routine of the house's other occupants.

According to Sumiteru's hours of work, Eiko slept, shopped and did the housework and cooking. Before long she had the impression that she was going to be happy; she soon got a feeling for the hill, for its plunging view down upon Nagasaki and its harbour, for its woods and its lights and colours. It was different from the smooth, long curves of the fields at Noda, but basically, it was the same: the earth and the sky were hers. There was only one dark cloud on her otherwise clear, untroubled horizon: the health of her husband. When summer came she realized for the first time how much the hot weather made him suffer; with the sweat glands of his back destroyed, he was unable to go to work under the sun; he remained all day, impatient, disconsolate in the house where he could benefit from the cooling mountain breezes. As summer tailed away to autumn he began to feel better. He took gladly to his work again and left early every morning to walk down the path and the 150 steps to the Asahi pier, board the ferry to Ohato pier and walk the few hundred metres up to the post office in Motohakati. His was a strenuous day, which included an hour or two at the *Hibakusha* Association's office up-town. The day over, he retraced his way home.

It was when he arrived that Eiko worried most. Her husband was at the limit of his strength. He never complained to her, but was always enthusiastic about his work, particularly with the *Hibakusha* movement. Nor had she ever any reason to complain to him. His needs were minimal. He did not eat much for fear of gaining weight – this could break the thin, tightly-stretched skin which covered his back and the burns on his legs and arms. He enjoyed a drink, but had to restrict himself for, once again, there was a risk of causing lesions in that fragile layer of skin. Sumiteru told his friends: 'My wife is lucky, since I hardly sweat nor eat, she has little work to do in the laundry and the kitchen.'

The day ended, Sumiteru would bid goodnight to Ji-san, to Mitzuyoshi and his wife; then he would accompany Eiko to their room to sleep together. Those were pleasant, intimate moments.

At the end of October, Eiko told her husband that she was expecting a baby. It was due to arrive at the beginning of July 1957. Sumiteru responded with a smile broader than usual. He was always a quiet, reserved person, but at this news there was no reason to hide his joy. It was what they both wanted. Sumiteru was thrilled, yet intensely frightened. As he well knew, he had received a massive dose of radiation. Would the baby be affected? Would it be deformed? mongoloid? microcephalic? blind? mentally retarded? lacking an arm or leg? stillborn? He knew of a child born to *hibakusha* parents without sight, of another without an arm and yet another with microcephaly, and assumed that these deformities were the result of the parents' exposure to radiation. Sumiteru was ceaselessly nagged by worry during the months to come. He never said a word to Eiko, but she also, knowing that Sumiteru had been exposed to radiation, never ceased to worry, day and night, for the baby.

The forty-six chromosomes in the human body are carriers of genes, which are themselves transmitters of hereditary characteristics. Chromosomes are highly susceptible to ionizing radiation which breaks them up. The fragments may join up with an identical chromosome; or they may not join up at all, remaining as acentric fragments. On the other hand they may join up with a different chromosome which then becomes aberrant. Aberrant chromosomes can be detected in the human body years later, which is to say that 'casualties' from radiation among the cells are not yet healed. While damage to the *hibakushas*' chromosomes was found to be in proportion to the radiation dose, the damage does not seem, up to the present, to have had any direct effect on their children, other than leaving both them and their parents with a stigma which marked them as different and apart from 'normal people'. The experts had so far found no positive evidence of genetic hazard for children born of *hibakusha* – 'second generation A-bombed' as the children were commonly called, or 'F.1.' – first filial generation. But doubts still lingered. There was a tendency outside the two atom-bombed cities not to accept them in marriage; a possibility existed of affected parents and their descendants not breeding to type.

In 1957 knowledge of the effects on F.1. *hibakusha* parents was still limited. Eiko's and Sumiteru's anxiety for their child was based on ignorance, on hearsay, and indeed on the fact that scores of young *hibakusha* had been refused in marriage. Tadashi was one. When a student in Tokyo he had been deeply in love with a girl who lived in the capital, but on hearing he was a *hibakusha* she had turned him down. Tadashi was later happily married to another girl. Similar dramas were frequent and continued into the second generation of the A-bombed, notwithstanding statistics which proved that the incidence of handicapped children born to *hibakusha* was no higher than with those born to the unexposed. Fears for *hibakushas'* children are not yet eradicated, however, nor can they be proved entirely irrational; it will take many more generations to determine the effects of the A-bomb on human genetics. Meanwhile, one thing is certain: nobody exposed to the atom bomb will ever be free of its consequences.

At the time, Eiko's and Sumiteru's fears for their child were understandable. Eiko even feared that her own anxiety might have a harmful effect on the baby. There was great joy, therefore, when a perfectly shaped little girl was born to Eiko on 5 July 1957.

Eiko accompanied by her mother had walked down to Doctor Kuniyoshi's private hospital the day before. The birth had been difficult and the baby, when born, had to be revived with an injection. Throughout Eiko's confinement Sumiteru had remained at home or at work in the office. In Japan husbands do not pace up and down outside their wife's maternity ward; that could bring bad luck. They stay away, and only on getting news of the baby's safe arrival does the husband hasten to the side of his wife and newborn child. At the sight of his first-born, Sumiteru could hardly contain his emotion. He took Eiko's hand and held it for some minutes. Then he planted a small kiss on the forehead of his daughter.

A week later the little girl – Sumei they called her, or Mei for short – returned in the arms of her mother to the house on the hill, accompanied by Eiko's mother who, as is customary in Japan, stayed on another three weeks or so with her daughter to allow her to rest. Then, thirty-three days after the birth, as custom required, Eiko and Sumiteru took the baby to the Yutoku Shrine at Togitsu, there to present her to the priest and receive his blessing.

Sumiteru remembered when, as a boy of thirteen, on New Year's Day 1942, he had gone to the great Suwa shrine. That day it had been with Obachan and Ji-san, to give thanks for Japan's stupendous run of victories and to pray for final victory in the New Year. How differently things had turned out. Today, 7 August, almost exactly twelve years after the atom bomb had nearly killed him, Sumiteru was standing at the altar beside his wife as they both prayed for their daughter's happiness.

With so much of her father's spare time taken up with the *Hibakusha* association, Sumei did not play a prominent part in Sumiteru's life. Yet in his mind, she and he were intimately associated. Hardly more than a child himself, he had been one of the thousands of boys and girls mutilated or slain by the atom bomb. The existence of his own child made him all the more passionately concerned with the *hibakushas*' avowed commitment, the abolition of nuclear weapons. Another thing, marriage and fatherhood had taken him one more step – a big one – away from the 'death and desolation' complex created by the atom bomb. Sumiteru at last was feeling a man again.

Few as the moments were that he could find to spend with his wife and daughter, Sumiteru never failed, at the end of even the most wearying day, in his role of husband and father. A strong, beautiful and intelligent child, Sumei was quick to exploit that gentle complicity between father and daughter. Sumiteru, as he teased her, hugged her, gave her piggy-back rides, he would sometimes wince from the pain from his wounds. But that did not deter him from his childish antics.

Sumei slept in her parents' room. The three of them made the beginnings of a tight little family, of which, one night in February 1959, a new member was conceived. Eiko announced the news to her husband at the beginning of March. As on the first occasion it filled them both with joy – which was all too soon darkened with fear.

Their first child was born without blemish; what of the next one? Might *it* not inherit some form of the contamination its father had suffered from the atom bomb? Sumiteru never spoke to Eiko of his fear, which was all the greater because his daughter had escaped unharmed. Could it be possible that the next child would be so fortunate?

Sumiteru kept a diary in which he daily recorded his fears

concerning the inherited effects of radiation on the child both he and Eiko longed for. One day he forgot to lock up his diary. Eiko came across it and began glancing through its pages. It was not long before she put it down, cold with fear for her expected baby. Her anguish increased as the days passed until, hardly able to bear it any longer, her thoughts turned to abortion – it was not an uncommon practice with mothers faced with the same problem, the *hibakusha* complex. It would free her from her anxiety, now amounting almost to terror; free the baby, too, if it were to be born handicapped, from an incomplete and probably miserable life. She could not bring herself to discuss her fear with Sumiteru. As with Sumei, it obsessed her and might well, she imagined, have some harmful pre-natal effect on the infant.

So Sumiteru and Eiko waited month after month, each possessed by the same fear yet too reserved, too timid of one another to share it; too alarmed lest, in revealing their fear, they might agree between themselves to abort the infant. They wanted so much to have a son; if the baby in her womb was a male, Eiko would never be able to forgive herself for aborting it, nor Sumiteru for allowing her to do so.

It was a chilly November morning, the twenty-first, when Eiko, taking her mother's arm, walked down the hill to the ferry. They crossed the harbour and at the Ohato pier took a taxi to the Teishin hospital for post office employees. She settled in, and in the early hours of the next day went into labour. This time all went smoothly and on 22 November at 6 a.m. she gave birth to a son.

At that moment Sumiteru was in bed at home – he was not due to go on duty until noon. There was no telephone in the house at the time, but as if by instinct he awoke at six o'clock, well before his normal time. He immediately threw on some clothes and, without spending time on breakfast, rushed down the hill, crossed the harbour and hurried on foot towards the hospital, to Eiko's bedside and the cradle of his newborn child – a fine little boy upon whom was no trace of blemish. Though he did his best to hide it, Sumiteru's emotion at seeing his son nearly overwhelmed him. The survival of the male line is to the Japanese more than a matter of pride – it is one of necessity. It struck Sumiteru as he looked down on his son and fondled the swaddled infant, as almost miraculous that he himself, who years ago had been given up for dead, had now succeeded in breathing life into another man, a child, innocent and immaculate, of his own poor mutilated flesh.

He took Eiko's hand and caressed it. Chosen as his wife by hazard when so much else in his life had been destroyed, she had bravely and faithfully partnered him in his act of creation, borne him these two lovely children. Into Sumiteru's life, to which he clung so precariously, she had brought an undreamed-of sense of fulfilment.

They called the boy Hideo. When a month or so later Sumiteru, carrying Sumei, and Eiko with Hideo in her arms, went to the Yutoku shrine to present the infant to the priest, Sumiteru gave up a fervent prayer of thanks.

24

It was not to Oba-chan's home that they returned. Amongst all
their private fears and doubts as Eiko waited for Hideo's birth,
one certainty emerged: they must move to a new house, a home
of their own. A little further down the hill from Oba-
chan's house, but still on her land, there was room to build.
Sumiteru's sister Keiko and his brother Teiji gladly agreed that
the plot should be made over to Sumiteru. Ji-san also con-
sented. Eiko's father was a builder, her brother a carpenter.
They both went to work and within two months, working day
and night, they finished the new house. It was there, after the
Yutoku shrine ceremony, that the family returned – to their
own home, a small but solidly built house of brick and wood
with a red-tiled roof – and with, of course, that sweeping view
across the hills and out over the city and harbour.

For some time nothing happened to disturb the peace of
their home. Eiko's hands were full with her children, who
seldom cried or disturbed the silence of the bedroom where
they slept with their parents. At night Sumiteru could recuper-
ate after his long day. He would go regularly to the A-bomb
hospital for tests, which spelt out no dramatic change for
better or for worse in the state of his health. But the open
wound in his back bothered him and, occasionally, it caused
him sharp pain. Then the pain passed and Sumiteru thought no
more of it – until the day in 1960, some six months after
Hideo's birth, when the doctor decided to have him x-rayed.
After examining the radiographs he spoke gravely to Sumiteru.
'The time has come when you will have to have major surgery.
This old wound of yours is the result of the intense burn on
your back. It has never healed because a deep scar has formed

in the tissue. Over the years it has developed into a bony tumour and should be removed. There's no reason to fear that it's malignant, but I must warn you: your blood-forming functions are still not normal and because of this I cannot say for certain that you will survive the operation. Do you agree we should go ahead?'

Without hesitation Sumiteru replied: 'Yes, please, I should like to have the tumour removed. But do you promise to keep it for me as a souvenir?' The doctor smiled. Sumiteru was obviously sure he would survive. All the same, when he returned home, he told Eiko the facts, then quietly said: 'The doctor thinks I may not survive. I don't believe him, but if he is right, then I should like the University hospital to have my body. They have done most of the tests for the last fifteen years and perhaps they will discover some hidden secret.' Two days later, Sumiteru, accompanied by Eiko, who carried the baby Hideo in her arms, was fetched by ambulance and taken down-town to the recently completed A-bomb hospital, intended specially for *hibakusha* cases. Eiko's mother took the little girl Sumei to her home in Noda.

Eiko had made these arrangements with but one idea in mind: she was deeply anxious for Sumiteru who was to be operated on that evening. Though hospital rules forbade relatives to spend the night there, she was determined to stay as close to his side as possible. She had friends among the other *hibakusha* patients, who told her: 'Don't worry. We will somehow hide you and the baby as if you were one of us. We will keep informed through a nurse we know in the operating theatre and let you know how Sumiteru-san is getting on.' So Eiko kept vigil. Towards midnight news came through that Sumiteru was out of the operation and doing well. Eiko was relieved; she slept a little but, waking early, waited impatiently for visiting hours.

Sumiteru was still sleepy from the anaesthetic, but vaguely he heard Eiko's voice: 'It's me, Sumi-san, and Hideo is here. We have been waiting close to you all night. We are happy you are well.' Then Eiko tried in simple language to make her husband understand her thoughts for him. 'I, who am not suffering the pain that you are, cannot feel how much it hurts you. But try to understand how much I feel for you in my heart. I am close to you, so are Hideo and Sumei. We shall come back to be with you, day after day, until you are well.' And so for a week, then another week, Eiko, carrying Hideo and holding Sumei by the hand, went to Sumiteru's bedside. He thought to himself: How good she is, and the little ones too. How much they have helped me.

After two weeks in hospital, Sumiteru was pronounced well. The doctor kept his promise. He gave Sumiteru the bony tumour, about three by two centimetres, which he had extracted from his back. Sumiteru kept it as a curio.

With Eiko carrying Hideo, and Sumiteru holding Sumei's hand, they walked unhurriedly back to their home on the hill. Sumiteru went back to work at the post office, but now, considering his recent operation and the ten or so years he had worked unrelentingly as a postman, he was given an office job. He was sorry to quit his daily runs on the red bicycle, delivering telegrams, but he realized that he simply had not the strength to continue.

The truth of this was confirmed not many months later. In early 1961 the ugly, disabling burns, which prevented him extending his left arm, began to give trouble. It was at the invitation of the East German Trades Union, the DFG, that Sumiteru's own union, SOHYO, the General Trades Union Council of Japan, sent him, with another *hibakusha* from Hiroshima, to a state hospital in East Berlin. It was Sumiteru's first contact with communists – not that he cared about anybody's political complexion. His conviction had always been that, notwithstanding their political differences, men have a basic common interest which, in simple terms, can be expressed by the word 'survival'.

During the three months he stayed in a private ward in East Germany, Sumiteru was well looked after; he found the German nurses even kinder than the Japanese. From them he learnt a little German. However, this agreeable but costly excursion brought him no relief. The German doctors agreed that it would need many operations to straighten out his left arm – with no guarantee of ultimate success. This was one of the reasons they decided not to operate. The other was that Sumiteru was not fit enough to undergo a series of operations; a sternum puncture, that painful stab in the chest with a hypodermic needle to extract bone-marrow, had proved that his blood-forming functions were still insufficient. Sumiteru's journey to Berlin had been pleasant but unprofitable. He returned to Nagasaki.

Though for fifteen years Sumiteru had suffered from the effects of the atom bomb which, as he well knew, would continue to the end of his days, this brave man refused to accept that he was chronically unwell. His main trouble was fatigue, the result of his many operations and the wound in his back which, since the operation, still gave him occasional sharp twinges of pain, suggesting that another tumour was forming in the place of the one extracted. These two factors were a drain on his strength, sometimes dragging him down into a state of nervous depression, sapping the energy he so much needed for his two passions – his family and the *hiba-kusha*.

No one could tell better than Sumiteru himself how greatly he had suffered, but this was no reason for him to consider himself a martyr; the world, he firmly believed, needed people who, through the example of their own suffering, could help it to move, if ever so slowly, towards a better understanding of human problems, and in his particular case, to the understanding that war and nuclear weapons cannot provide an answer to them. Sumiteru was a Buddhist, though he did not pray as a good Buddhist should. He believed, as a Buddhist, that violence of any kind was wrong, but deeds, he thought, were more effective than prayers. He put himself freely at the disposal of anyone – school-children, journalists and a wide variety of people concerned by the atom bomb – who came to question him. He told them quietly of its cruel consequences upon his own mind and body, upon his family and all the 400,000 *hibakusha* contaminated by the bomb and still surviving. He wanted a world safe and clean enough for human beings, especially children, to live in. A world divided by political ideologies and the lust of a few men – and women – for power seemed to him like hell, nothing less.

On leaving hospital he went back to his old routine – the early rising, the descent down the path and the 150 steps, the ferry across the harbour and the walk uphill to the post office in Motohakati-machi. In the evening he took the same well-trodden road, only this time ending more steeply uphill, with those 150 steps back to his home. He was used to this tread-mill existence and when, at the end of the day, his physical endurance began to wilt, he somehow made a mental switch to 'automatic' – his legs and his lungs functioned without his consciously willing them. They carried him up the narrow path, up the steps, until he stumbled to the front door, slipped off his shoes and crossed the threshold of his dear home, where he flopped into a low chair and his family came to him.

Sumiteru's greatest joy was his family. His loyalty to the post office service was naturally unconditional, since it provided his only means of existence, but he had no ambition for promotion. He lived for his family and the *hibakusha*. They alone inspired his fight to surmount his physical handicap.

Sumiteru had on several occasions and for long periods been on close terms with death. He was not afraid of dying. It appeared to him to be less painful, more decisive than his daily struggle against ill-health, coupled with the demands of his job. But as long as he lived he gladly accepted the monotonous, inescapable fight for his own survival. And as long as his own survival was assured, he would give all of himself to his family and the *hibakusha*. He saw them as one, as the sole object of his existence. This dual loyalty was to raise an unexpected problem with the children.

25

When Sumei was three, she often took a bath or a shower with
her father. It was fun splashing water at him and he in turn
enjoyed giving her rudimentary swimming lessons. She of
course saw his naked body, and found nothing unusual in the
shiny, pink, irregular skin covering his back, in the smooth,
parchment-like surface of his left arm and parts of his legs.
That, she imagined, was how her father was made; with his
clothes on he looked just like any other man she had ever seen.
She loved him as he was.

When, in 1962, Hideo was nearly three, he joined his father
and sister in the bathroom. His reaction to his father's naked
body was exactly the same as Sumei's had been. He noticed
those big patches of skin which were different from the rest,
but supposed that all other men were more or less like that
beneath their clothes.

In the summer of 1963, when Sumei was six and Hideo not
far from his fourth birthday, Eiko and Sumiteru took them for
the first time to the seaside. There were three beaches they
particularly liked and could reach by bus: Fukuda, Miyazuri
and Kawahara. Tobo-no-hama, where Sumiteru had some
years ago made that famous gesture, stripping off his shirt and
exposing his back to everyone's view, was being spoilt by
construction work which was reclaiming most of the beach
from the sea.

Fukuda beach was the nearest and the most pleasant, with
its swimming pool and its broad stretch of sand washed by the
waters of the East China Sea. It was there one day in mid-
August, that they disembarked from the blue and silver bus.
Sumiteru, carrying Hideo, and Eiko, holding Sumei's hand,

picked their way through the crowds idling on the beach, chatting, basking, picnicking. 'Come on, Mei, try to keep up,' Eiko kept repeating to the little girl, who was straining at her mother's hand, deeply intrigued by all those half-naked bodies. Apart from her father, she had never seen people with so little on, and she stared unashamedly at each smooth-skinned, sunburnt body as she passed by. Sumiteru and his family at last found a vacant patch of sand for themselves.

'Quick!' exclaimed Sumei, 'let's go into the sea.'

'Yes, quick, into the sea,' echoed Hideo, who loved the water even more than his sister.

Fat, billowing clouds drifted across the sky, sweeping the beach with fleeting shade. It was not the kind of intense sunlight in which Sumiteru felt he must wear his shirt for protection. At the children's cry: 'Let's go and swim!' he pulled off his shirt, took each one by the hand and led them towards the water. After a few paces he felt Sumei's small hand tugging at his. She broke loose from his grasp and ran back to her mother. A pace or two further, Hideo, panicked by his sister's flight, did the same. He too ran back to his mother to find Sumei in her arms, crying. Hideo immediately started to cry, too, not really knowing why. Sumiteru walked back to Eiko, who was doing her best to console the children. 'What's the matter?' he asked her. 'Why all these tears?'

'Put your shirt on, Sumi-san, and sit down,' she told him. 'It's very simple really. The children never worried about your poor burnt body until today, when they see how different and – forgive me – how frightening it looks next to all these healthy, bronzed people on the beach. It has shocked Sumei. Hideo is only crying because she is. Please talk to them in your own quiet way and leave me to make sure later that they have understood.' It was one of those moments when Eiko rose unfailingly to the occasion.

Sumiteru tried to hide his chagrin. How often before had he experienced this painful rejection, been considered unclean, apart, because of his scars. Now his own children were actually running away from him, terrified.

Without hurrying he put his shirt on again, buttoning it by a single button, slowly rolling up each sleeve just above the elbow. He must at least leave visible to the children as much of his scarred body as they could accept. The problem was his back. Distressed as he felt, he was determined to talk them round into accepting it too. 'Now, Mei,' he spoke gently to his daughter. 'Stop crying. And you, Hideo, what are you crying about? You want to be a man, don't you? Men don't cry – anyway,' he added under his breath, 'not all that often.' He put his arms round both children. 'Listen to me,' he said. 'I am going to tell you something. If you don't understand, Mama will explain later.

'First, think of the fun we've had at home in the bath and under the shower. You never cried then when you saw me; no, you laughed and we played. Now you are crying because you have compared my body with the fine bronzed bodies of the people around us. But that's no reason for you to be afraid of me. You know I am your father, who loves you and who is there to take care of you and your mother. My body when I was small used to be just like yours and all these other peoples.' Then, when I was a boy of sixteen, a thing called an atom bomb made a very terrible fire in Nagasaki and burnt down most of the city. Thousands of people, some as young as you, were killed and burnt. I was one of them. None of us had done any wrong. The wrong was done by other men against us. People like me are called *hibakusha*; we are the ones who were hurt by that fiery atom bomb but are still alive. We want everyone else to see how badly it wounded and burnt our bodies and to listen to us, because only we can tell them how awful it is to be hit by an atom bomb.'

Sumei and Hideo had stopped crying and were listening intently to their father. Sumei at least was getting the gist of his words; Eiko would explain the rest to them later. 'Now listen, my little ones,' Sumiteru went on, 'I'm going to take off my shirt again so that when I walk through these crowds in the water, anybody who wants to can see what the atom bomb did to a young boy and thousands of other poor people, many of them babies like you. It's not my fault that I have such ugly scars and so I am not ashamed of them. So try to be brave, both of you, and stay with me. There are thousands more *hibakusha* like me; we want people to know all about the dreadful thing that was done to us so that they will never allow it to happen again.

'One last thing. The motto of our city is, "Peace from Nagasaki". It might be better to say: "Prayers from Nagasaki, that ours shall be the last atomic bomb", or something like that.'

Sumiteru kissed each one of them, unbuttoned his shirt and took it off, 'Now, come on,' he said to the children, 'and don't be afraid.' He took them each by the hand; this time they followed him willingly. Eiko with her placid smile watched them as they walked among the sunbathers. Then they ran across the sand and went splashing into the clean, warm waters of the East China Sea.

EPILOGUE

When, thirty-seven years after the atomic bomb, I met Doctor Tatsuichiro Akizuki, Masato Araki, Senzi Yamaguti, Yukie Tsuji, Tadashi Kokurawa, Sid Lawrence, Sumiteru and many other *hibakusha*, they appeared outwardly to be in reasonably good health. Yet every one of them was in some measure suffering from the after-effects. Even the resilient Doctor Akizuki, still director of the St Francis hospital, admitted that every time August comes round, he is aware of that strange malaise that affects all *hibakusha*. He tries to ignore it and upbraids other *hibakusha* for not doing the same.

Masato Araki, until recently vice-director of the Nagasaki International Cultural Hall and A-bomb Museum, has over the years become innured to the horror. But memories of his personal tragedy are as vivid as ever: his flight from the burning city to take refuge on the hill, where, through the rest of the day and the following night, he prayed, in vain, for his father's safety.

Yukie Tsuji is a small, vivacious lady, and while the radiant-heat scars on her face and arms remain indelible, they do not detract from her lively personality. As a founder-member of the Nagasaki Young Women's *Hibakusha* Association, she says that although the passing years are steadily thinning the ranks of the *Hibakusha*, those who remain, ever conscious as they are of their unique experience, will never give up their fight for nuclear disarmament and peace.

As founder of the joint Association of Young Men and Women *Hibakusha* of Nagasaki, Senzi Yamaguti is still extremely active as its president. The effects of the A-bomb go far deeper than the marks it branded so cruelly on his skin. Struck down so early in his life, he believes, to say the least, that the bomb was a crime against children. It has left him with an implacable hatred of war and militarism.

Tadashi, too, thinks that, even though it was war-time and that it has always been claimed that the A-bomb averted the death of hundreds of thousands more innocent people, it was still a crime to use it, for it wiped out so many thousands of innocent people, including his parents and six of his young cousins, and caused permanent bodily harm to thousands of others. He was one, and for the rest of his life he has been unable to take on anything but the lightest work. Apart from the sense of failure this gives him, there have been other psychological effects. Since the day of the A-bomb, he has been unable to bear the smell of baked wheat and potatoes. Nor can he face one of the most popular dishes in Japan – *mezashi*, dried fish. They all revive memories of the stench that pervaded Nagasaki during the aftermath of the A-bomb.

Tadashi's twenty-year-old daughter, Yasuko, was one of the brightest pupils at the Junshin High School. When, aged about twelve, Yasuko discovered that she was the daughter of a *hibakusha*, she became haunted by the fear of contracting leukaemia or some other disease said to threaten 'second generation A-bomb victims'. In time, she put the fear out of her mind, as she did the prejudice held against the children of *hibakusha*. Not all children of *hibakusha* have been able to convince themselves as Yasuko has done.

The view held by Sid Lawrence on whether the A-bomb was a crime or not, are, like Senzi's and Tadashi's, influenced by his own experience. While the A-bomb was an instrument of mass extermination from which he barely escaped, it probably, he thinks, saved him and other prisoners of war from a mass killing at the hands of the Japanese. Sid was repatriated to England; during his 'de-briefing', he was shown a list of prisoners held in Japan, believed dead, and asked if he could identify any of the names. Spotting his own, he wrote against it: 'Not on your nelly – alive, just.'

It was the literal truth. For years Sid was to suffer from a variety of distressing physical and psychological disorders. Swallowing salt, spoonfuls at a time, gave him some relief. His terrifying nightmares in time became more rare, but even now he sometimes wakes up, crying inconsolably. He cannot explain exactly why, but is certain that it must stem from the unearthly horror of the A-bomb, which will for ever haunt him. It was the atom bomb, he realizes, that, while it brought death and lasting misery to so many, spared Sid to return to England, there to rebuild his life with Irene, his wife, and their son. But the question keeps nagging him: 'What am I doing alive? I should have died with all those thousands of others.'

In his home on the hillside overlooking Nagasaki, I talked, night after night, to Sumiteru. As I listened to him, I had the feeling that there was something saintly about him. He related his martyrdom – it was nothing less – with perfect humility and occasionally even with humour. He harbours no rancour against his aggressors. His one concern, apart from his daily job, is to fight without sparing himself for the *hibakushas'* cause: to rid the world of nuclear weapons. While he appreciates arguments for the nuclear deterrent, he fervently believes that mankind deserves better, can do better, than to continue cowering under the perpetual threat of nuclear annihilation.

As Eiko told me, her husband devotes his life to helping others, both in the Peace Movement and outside it. His sister, Keiko, and Teiji, his brother, often come to him for advice; his father Sadamachi (now in his nineties) too. Sumiteru's grandfather Ji-san, who had stuck to him so loyally, died peacefully in 1970.

Sumiteru cannot say his life has been a happy one; he was too badly hurt in his youth. But there have been great compensations. Eiko's devotion has enabled him to make a success out of his ruined youth. Their son Hideo, now a student at Nagasaki University, and their daughter Sumei and her two beautiful children, are the overwhelming proof that Sumiteru, who had so nearly succumbed to the monstrous life-destroying power of the atom bomb, has finally succeeded in creating new life. Out of his survival comes his unyielding opposition to the further use of nuclear weapons. Sumiteru and his *hibakusha* friends know better than anyone else in the world what they are talking about. Only they have actually been A-bombed and suffered the consequences.

Eiko worries about her husband's health, especially when August and the anniversary of the A-bomb comes round, with the heavy pressure on him by the international media, by numerous peace movements and individual enquirers. In 1978, a new and serious problem arose connected with Sumiteru's burns. Yet it was in that year that he decided to travel to Europe and the United States, to spread his message. The demands on his limited forces were severely increased; so was Eiko's concern for his health. She told me it is like holding a time-bomb in her hand, never knowing when it would go off. Sumiteru himself, while well aware of his own frailty, remains astonishingly resistant and philosophical. He is convinced, as always, that some people, like him, are born to greater sufferings than others; that suffering has a purpose. He is far too modest to consider himself, on this account, as a martyr. All he wishes, as a *hibakusha*, as one who suffered the abominable effects of nuclear warfare, is to preach, far and wide, for the rest of his days: 'Peace from Nagasaki. May the second atom bomb be the last.'

BIBLIOGRAPHY

The Rising Sun, by John Toland, Random House, New York, 1970.

The Nuclear Barons, by Peter Prince and James Spiegelman, Michael Joseph, London, 1982.

Hiroshima and Nagasaki, the physical, medical and social effects of the Atomic Bombing. Edited by the Committee for the compilation of materials on damage caused by the atomic bomb in Hiroshima and Nagasaki; Hutchinson, London, 1981 (originally published in Japanese by Iwanami Shoten, Tokyo, 1979).

Nagasaki 1945, by Tatsuichiro Akizuki, Quartet Books, London, 1981.

Journal of Radiation Research, The Japan Radiation Research Society, Chiba, Japan, 1975.

The Delayed Effects of Radiation, Radiation Effects Research Foundation, Nagasaki, 1980.

Hiroshima-Nagasaki, a pictorial record (and numerous other documents), Hiroshima-Nagasaki Publishing Committee, Tokyo, 1978-1982.